POETICA 10

VICTOR HUGO
The Distance, The Shadows

BY HARRY GUEST

POETRY

Arrangements, 1968
The Cutting-Room, 1970
A House Against the Night, 1976
English Poems, 1976
Lost and Found, 1983
Coming to Terms, 1994
So Far, 1998
A Puzzling Harvest, 2002
(*Collected Poems 1955–2000*)

TRANSLATION

Post-War Japanese Poetry, 1972
(*with Lynn Guest and Kajima Shôzô*)
Versions, 1999

FICTION

Days, 1978
Lost Pictures, 1991

NON-FICTION

Another Island Country, 1970
Mastering Japanese, 1989
Traveller's Literary Companion to Japan, 1994
The Artist on the Artist, 2000

VICTOR HUGO

The Distance, The Shadows

SELECTED POEMS

TRANSLATED BY

HARRY GUEST

ANVIL PRESS POETRY

First published in 1981
New edition published in 2002
by Anvil Press Poetry Ltd
Neptune House 70 Royal Hill London SE10 8RF
www.anvilpresspoetry.com

This book is published with financial assistance
from The Arts Council of England

Designed and set in Monotype Janson by Anvil

ISBN 0 85646 345 0

A catalogue record for this book
is available from the British Library

TO MY FORMER PUPILS

French Contents

from *Odes*, 1822
Au vallon de Cherizy 155
Le matin 157

from *Les Orientales*, 1829
L'enfant 157
Attente 158
Rêverie 159

from *Les Feuilles d'automne*, 1831
Soleils couchants, vi 160
A un voyageur 160
'Lorsque l'enfant paraît...' 163
'Oh! qui que vous soyez...' 164

from *Les Chants du crépuscule*, 1835
from Napoléon ii 166
Sur le bal de l'Hôtel de Ville 166
'L'aurore s'allume...' 168
'Puisque j'ai mis ma lèvre...' 169

from *Les Voix intérieures*, 1837
A Albert Dürer 170
'A quoi je songe...?' 171

from *Les Rayons et les Ombres*, 1840
Oceano nox 172
Nuits de juin 173
Tristesse d'Olympio 174

from *Les Châtiments*, 1853
Le chant de ceux qui s'en vont sur mer 179
Le chasseur noir 180
L'expiation, i 182
Souvenir de la nuit du 4 183
'Sonnez, sonnez toujours...' 185

English Contents

PREFACE   13

from *Odes*, 1822
  In the Valley of Cherizy   27
  Morning   30

from *Les Orientales*, 1829
  The Boy   31
  Waiting   33
  Reverie   34

from *Les Feuilles d'automne*, 1831
  Sunset   35
  To a Traveller   36
  The Child Appears   39
  'Whoever you may be ...'   42

from *Les Chants du crépuscule*, 1835
  Tomorrow   44
  Concerning the Ball at the Hôtel de Ville   45
  'Dawn is igniting ...'   47
  'Since I have placed my lip ...'   48

from *Les Voix intérieures*, 1837
  To Albrecht Dürer   49
  My Thoughts   51

from *Les Rayons et les Ombres*, 1840
  Night on the Ocean   53
  June Nights   55
  Olympio: His Sadness   56

from *Les Châtiments*, 1853
  The Song of Those Who Go to Sea   63
  The Huntsman of the Night   64
  The Retreat from Moscow   67
  A Recollection of the Night of 4 December 1851   70
  'Let all the bugles ...'   73

from *Les Contemplations*, 1856

I

Mes deux filles	185
Vieille chanson du jeune temps	186
L'enfance	187
Unité	188

II

Premier mai	188
Le rouet d'Omphale	189
Lettre	190
'Viens! – une flûte invisible …'	191
Paroles dans l'ombre	191
Un soir que je regardais le ciel	192

III

Écrit au bas d'un crucifix	194
Écrit sur la plinthe d'un bas-relief antique	194
'La clarté du dehors …'	195
'L'enfant, voyant l'aïeule …'	196
'J'aime l'araignée …'	196

IV

'Elle avait pris ce pli …'	197
'Quand nous habitions tous ensemble …'	198
Veni, vidi, vixi	199
'Demain, dès l'aube …'	200

V

Paroles sur la dune	201
Pasteurs et troupeaux	202

VI

Ce que c'est que la mort	204
Nomen, numen, lumen	204

from *La Légende des siècles*, 1ère série, 1859

Le sacre de la femme	205
La conscience	210
Booz endormi	211
Première rencontre du Christ avec le tombeau	214

from *Les Contemplations*, 1856

I

My Two Daughters   74
Old Song of my Young Days   75
Childhood   77
Unity   78

II

The First of May   79
Queen Omphalé's Spinning-Wheel   80
Letter   82
'Come – an unseen flute . . .'   84
Words Spoken in the Shadows   85
One Evening When I Was Looking at the Sky   86

III

Written Beneath a Crucifix   88
On the Plinth of an Ancient Bas-Relief   89
'The bright air outside . . .'   90
'A little girl . . .'   92
'Spider, nettle, loathed . . .'   93

IV

'She formed the habit . . .'   95
'On our hills of the past . . .'   96
Veni, Vidi, Vixi   98
'At dawn, tomorrow . . .'   100

V

Words Spoken on the Dunes   101
Shepherds and Their Flocks   103

VI

What Death Is   105
Nomen, Numen, Lumen   106

from *La Légende des siècles*, first series, 1859
The Consecration of Woman   107
Conscience   115
Boaz Asleep   117
Christ's First Encounter with the Tomb   120

La rose de l'infante 216
Après la bataille 222

from *Les Chansons des rues et des bois*, 1865
Ordre du jour de floréal 222
Rosa fâchée 223
Saison des semailles. Le soir 224
'Les enfants lisent, troupe blonde...' 224
'Va-t'en, me dit la bise...' 226
Pendant une maladie 226

from *L'Année terrible*, 1872
A l'enfant malade pendant le siège 228
A qui la faute? 229

from *Toute la lyre*, 1888
A Théophile Gautier 231

from *La Légende des siècles*, 11me série, 1877
Orphée 233
Après les fourches caudines 234

from *L'Art d'être grand-père*, 1877
Fenêtres ouvertes 235
'Jeanne songeait...' 235

from *Les Quatre vents de l'esprit*, 1881
A ma fille Adèle 236

The Rose in the Infanta's Hand 123
After the Battle 131

from *Les Chansons des rues et des bois*, 1865
Orders for the Day: Late Spring 132
Rosa's Angry 133
The Sower 134
'The children read . . .' 135
Onset of Winter 137
During an Illness 138

from *L'Année terrible*, 1872
For Jeanne, Ill During the Siege of Paris 140
Whose Fault Is It? 141

from *Toute la lyre*, 1888
To Théophile Gautier 143

from *La Légende des siècles*, second series, 1877
Orpheus 146
After the Caudine Forks 147

from *L'Art d'être grand-père*, 1877
Open Windows: Early Morning 149
Grand-daughter 150

from *Les Quatre vents de l'esprit*, 1881
To My Daughter Adèle 151

NOTES 237
BIBLIOGRAPHY 241
CHRONOLOGICAL TABLE 243
INDEX OF FRENCH TITLES 247
INDEX OF ENGLISH TITLES 249

I should like to express my gratitude to the Arts Council of Great Britain for a grant that made the completion of this project possible; to Robin Hone, then Headmaster, and to the Bursar and Governors of Exeter School for their kindness in arranging a sabbatical term; to Ruth and David James for their patience in reading many of these versions and for their valuable comments on them; and to my wife who put up with four months of my being home to lunch.

H.G.

Preface

THE ROMANTIC MOVEMENT in literature occurred somewhat later in France than in England or Germany and had an even more revolutionary flavour. It could with some justification be claimed that the storming of the Bastille and the subsequent course of the French Revolution manifested many of the extremer aspects of romanticism – iconoclasm, rejection of the immediate past, interest in the individual, fascination with the murky underside of human nature – as well as, at least on paper, that passion for subjective freedom that was to characterize a great deal of romantic writing from Kleist to Huysmans. However, it was not until the 1820s that anything resembling a French romantic movement became crystallized.

In art of course clear-cut divisions never exist. Rousseau in his eccentric views on education and his Social Contract ('Man is born free and everywhere he is in chains') and Beaumarchais with his tilts at the hereditary power of the aristocrats had already heralded several of the themes that were to be associated with the romantic movement. Indeed by 1805 the dark genius of Chateaubriand was giving more than a hint of the storms that were to come with his sense of brooding individuality and his taste for forbidden fruit. Even so, the prevailing mood that reigned in France after the defeat of Napoleon was formal, eighteenth-century and unchanged. Art was supposed to conform with certain tenets and these, said the traditionalists, were sacrosanct. The alexandrine had to have a caesura after the sixth syllable; enjambement (used in fact so supply by Racine) was forbidden; there was a limited vocabulary available for poetry and certain words were literally unmentionable. 'Mouchoir' was among them. It was Shakespeare's use of a handkerchief as a plot-point in *Othello* that most aggrieved the purists and convinced them, more than ever, that the Anglo-Saxons were a barbarous lot.

When, in 1854, Victor Hugo looked back on the literary battles that had been waged in his youth he made an explicit connection between the act of freeing language from the confines of 'good taste' and the liberation of thought itself. He claimed to have been a true revolutionary, to have 'put a red cap on the dictionary' and proved that there were no 'special' words for poetry thus making the vocabulary of literature properly egalitarian and ridding words of any 'class-consciousness' they were held to contain. He identified the 'new' poet with Danton and Robespierre, going so far as to claim that he and his contemporaries in the 1820s had recreated the atmosphere of 1789 with their assault on the academic bastions where at that time the traditionalists were ensconced, powerful and middle-aged. The romantics were different, free and above all young. Led by Gautier in his pink waistcoat they all rallied in February 1830 to show their support for a play in verse the very opening couplet of which contained an enjambement – Hugo's verbal gauntlet flung at the complacent feet of the literary establishment. A riot broke out in the theatre and at the end of its brief tumultuous run *Hernani* proved that romanticism had arrived.

II

HUGO'S CAREER up to that moment had not been remarkable for upsetting apple-carts. Indeed his relations both with Louis XVIII and Charles X had been cordial and profitable. Then, in August 1829, the latter banned the play *Marion de Lorme* apparently finding that Hugo's portrayal of Louis XIII reflected unflatteringly upon himself. The author, piqued, refused the subsequent offer of a royal pension. This was to be the first of many brushes with authority.

In 1830 Hugo was twenty-eight. His father who had died two years before was a professional soldier. Napoleon promoted him to the rank of general and gave him the title of count. Victor grew up knowing the grandiloquence and ultimately the humiliation of the First Empire. General Hugo was a native of eastern France and his wife, born in Nantes, was of Breton stock. With his delight in opposites Hugo was to value highly this geographic discrepancy in his blood. The parents in fact soon became estranged and Victor led a nomadic life with his two brothers, in Spain and elsewhere, before settling in Paris where Victor especially excelled in Latin and philosophy. He soon decided to make literature his career though he was a gifted and original painter and draughtsman who experimented successfully with romantic effects in different visual media – as well as providing startlingly effective illustrations as a commentary on his written works both in prose and verse.

The poems in his first books, the two collections of *Odes* and the later *Ballades* published between 1822 and 1826 show the poet already a superb musician in full technical control of his material and fascinated by the possibilities in linguistic experiment. At this time he was a passionate royalist and an ardent Catholic. Although he later abandoned the Church he remained a theist all his life – 'To believe is hard,' he said; 'not to believe is impossible.' His political views moved more slowly away from his initial support for monarchy until he ended up loathing kings in any shape or form.

These early collections contain, in among the public poetry, love-poems as well as analyses of his developing state of mind. In each piece he gives full rein to his marvellously *concrete* imaginative powers. There is from the outset never any doubt as to what it is Hugo is describing – the emotional landscape is precisely delineated with each image, however striking or bizarre, accurately in place and portrayed with the clarity of a master.

Hugo's defence of the romantic movement written in 1854 nearly a quarter of a century after the great battle had been fought and won is true in literary practice – from the start Hugo's vocabulary was richly appropriate to whatever theme captured his attention – although the political theory is very much the result of hindsight. It is interesting that Hugo's romanticism in the 1820s was preoccupied with the rights of one individual – Hugo – to write as he wished. The other side of the romantic coin – concern for the rights of man in general – was to come with full maturity when Hugo became an international crusader in the cause of justice.

III

AFTER MUCH OPPOSITION from her father Adèle Foucher became his wife in 1822. They had four children after the early death of their firstborn Léopold. Victor, whose parents had both conducted long extra-marital affairs showed himself to be capable of intense love but not, except in short bursts, of fidelity.

Adèle too became physically estranged from her husband when she fell in love with his friend Sainte-Beuve. Hugo's poetry, at this time especially, sprang vitally as a diary from his immediate experiences and so it is not surprising to find in the same book, *Les Feuilles d'automne* (1831), both the marvellous celebration of friendship and family-life in 'Lorsque l'enfant paraît...' and, in 'Oh! qui que vous soyez...', an example of the agonizing jealousy he felt when his wife was with the man who had been his best friend.

This book is the first in which it is entirely apparent that a great poet has arrived, though there are fine things in *Les Orientales* which appeared two years earlier. This volume, a favourite of Gide's, was hailed by those members of the romantic movement – the so-called 'picturesque' school – who believed that the exotic and dramatic (or melodramatic) were the proper concern of the artist. However, when in a poem like 'L'enfant' Hugo treats a cherished theme – that of childhood – he is also adumbrating that compassion for the victims of oppression that is to characterize so much of his later work.

IV

IN 1832 HIS PLAY *Le Roi s'amuse*, adapted in 1851 as *Rigoletto*, was banned by Louis-Philippe. Hugo again rejected the offer of a pension from a different king. His next play, *Lucrèce Borgia*, performed in 1833, is important because the small part of Princess Negroni was played by Juliette Drouet who became his mistress, companion and loyal friend and who, until her death nearly fifty years later, acted as a kind of unpaid secretary copying out all his works in longhand. After he had rapturously celebrated their love in the poem 'Puisque j'ai mis ma lèvre...' (unambiguously dated 1 January 1835, 12:30 a.m.), they stayed frequently in the valley of the Bièvre and it is a return to this landscape that provoked the great ode 'Tristesse d'Olympio' in which Hugo magnificently attempts to come to terms with the passage of time, to replace experience with memory and find what consolation he can in the fact of being mortal.

He was by now a successful playwright and novelist as well as France's leading poet. Increasingly he was becoming involved in public life, notably in his untiring campaign against the death-penalty. Books, pamphlets, articles of all kinds poured from his pen. Then his play *Les Burgraves* failed spectacularly in 1843 and Hugo gave up the drama. *Hernani* had cleared the air by proving to French audiences that the hallowed unities of time, place and action were not essential ingredients of a play. Many of his dramas contain fine speeches. There are memorable theatrical effects. But Hugo's plays are more literary history than living drama though, in 1954, Gérard Philipe was radiantly successful in a revival of *Ruy Blas*, perhaps the most rounded of all Hugo's plays.

Hugo was indeed a major dramatist – but, paradoxically, only in the domain of his lyric or epic poetry. He had an intense feeling for dramatic contrast, light and shade, the clash and reverberation of opposites. He knew how to narrate spell-bindingly and make the simplest character leap vitally from the page. Like so many other nineteenth-century figures of genius – Dickens, Turner, Tolstoy – he had overflowing energy, an immense capacity for work and three-dimensional powers of concentration. Above all, Hugo found verse a natural means of expression and part of his astonishing strength stems from his ability to charge the colloquial with poetic importance, to make the direct statement carry pathos, colour and weight.

In September 1843 his elder daughter Léopoldine and her husband were drowned at the mouth of the Seine. The poems Hugo wrote about his dead daughter are among the most moving in the language. Like many other romantic poets Hugo had a special regard for the sanctity of childhood and he had the imaginative power to see, without sentimentality, into the minds of children even when they only seem to appear as characters in poems written in the first person.

v

WHEN IN 1848 the régime of Louis-Philippe was toppled Hugo threw himself wholeheartedly into public life – first as a deputy for the 'right' but, as the President of the Second Republic, Louis-Napoléon, nephew of the Emperor, moved steadily towards the organization of a police-state, Hugo found his human and political ideals more and more at variance until he fixed himself permanently as a man of the 'left', a democrat and a fervent anti-royalist. With his two sons he ran an opposition newspaper and when in 1851 the President proclaimed himself Emperor, Hugo left France vowing not to return until Napoléon-le-petit, as he dubbed him, was removed from the throne. The 'Emperor' was henceforward in charge of Jericho and history was waiting until Hugo/Joshua could find the opportunity to blow the trumpet of salvation.

During the long years of exile – for he refused the amnesty offered in 1859 – first in Belgium, then in Jersey, finally Guernsey, Hugo's visionary powers expanded. He had proved himself a major lyric poet in his collections *Les Chants du crépuscule* (1835), *Les Voix intérieures* (1837) and *Les Rayons et les Ombres* (1840). He sounded with success so many notes – tenderness, mystery, rhetoric, bereavement, lament for times gone by as well as bright celebration of the new. He had an almost pantheistic awareness of the natural world – widely and unconventionally so, for wolves are included in his joyous welcome to spring, 'Premier mai', and 'J'aime l'araignée...' shows sympathy with the unloved members of nature. He relished the grotesque for its own sake, as yet another manifestation of life's richness. He was luminously capable of observing human behaviour, perceiving always a greater significance behind and beyond the mere evidence of the senses. With *Les Châtiments* (1853, though not published in France until 1870) the note of controlled fury is added – hatred for tyranny and all its works, for the cruelty in the heart of man, for the organizers of the *coup d'état* in 1851 when a little boy of seven was shot down in the street – an event Hugo witnessed and which he commemorated in his grim 'Souvenir de la nuit du 4'.

His dislike for Napoleon III is based on such events. In his attitude to Napoleon I however there is a certain ambiguity. Several of his poems are concerned with the heroism of his father and uncle during their campaigns with the first emperor. In his justly famous description of the retreat from Moscow, Napoleon is seen as a tragic figure, larger than life, commanding and deserving loyalty. At the same time he is an emperor and the words *king* and *emperor* now have for Hugo the overtones of *evil* and *oppressor*.

IN 1856, IN EXILE, arguably his greatest work appeared – *Les Contemplations*, a work both beautifully and logically organized as a whole. Its six books are divided in two by the death of Léopoldine – this is why, though appearing thirteen years after her death, many of the poems have dates prior to 1843. In the first three books he includes love-poems, nature-poems, recollections of past battles, past achievements. In the second half he confronts the problems of the grave and peers beyond this world to the mysteries of eternal life and the realms of the infinite. These works are unfortunately often too long for inclusion in a selection of this kind but shorter poems like 'Nomen, numen, lumen' or 'Ce que c'est que la mort' show the way he throws his imagination further than the confines of experience while still retaining that innate sense of the concrete, of the possible, of what can be described.

Even the apocalyptic poems in *Les Contemplations* are, in fact, examples of the lyric. Hugo now embarked wholeheartedly on the epic. For the rest of his long life his main preoccupation in verse was with the three series of *La Légende des siècles* which had as their staggering schema nothing less than the history of mankind from the dawn of time to the nineteenth century and beyond. The collection remained, as was perhaps inevitable, unfinished at his death but it is crammed with unforgettable triumphs – his picture of Cain fleeing from the eye of conscience, Philip II's hubris as he envisages the success of the Armada, and perhaps, literally, most miraculous of all, the breathless glory that suspended the universe when Eve 'felt a stirring in her womb'.

A good example of his delight in chiaroscuro, in balance and contrast and dramatic comparison is provided by the fact that, while working on *La Légende des siècles*, he brought out a collection of lyric poems in short-lined form, *Les Chansons des rues et des bois*, published in Brussels in 1865. This is a fascinating book, quirky, colloquial, containing a freshness of skill and joy in sheer technical inventiveness – even the poems recording a time when he was seriously ill have a wry toughness about them that is the reverse of morbid.

IN 1870, NINETEEN YEARS after he had gone into exile, Hugo returned to celebrate the downfall of Napoleon III and the proclamation of the Third Republic. He was given a hero's welcome and became once more involved enthusiastically in French political life. His diary kept during the siege of Paris is compulsive reading – prices soar, there's drift-ice on the Seine, rats are devoured, shells fall on the city and Hugo is so much an admired public figure that the zoo authorities send him a haunch of antelope. Poems about this siege, the events of the Franco-Prussian war and the upheavals of the Commune appeared in *L'Année terrible*.

The hated Empire was shattered but France had lost a war. In the second series of *La Légende des siècles* Hugo summed up the feelings of defeat in a poem 'Après les fourches caudines', remarkable in the way, although cast as a historical piece, its Roman setting becomes perfectly transparent and the reader sees two eras simultaneously as the poet in the foreground watches a squad of dragoons canter past him near Longchamp.

His son Charles died in 1871, leaving two children, Georges and Jeanne. In his seventies Victor Hugo was able once more to study childhood at first hand, assembling his charming observations in *L'Art d'être grand-père*.

Mme Hugo died in 1868. His two sons predeceased their father, his surviving daughter was mentally unstable and, in 1883, Juliette Drouet died. Two years later almost to the day Victor Hugo died at the age of 83. In his novel *Les Déracinés* Barrès gave a stirring account of the funeral a sorrowing but appreciative nation accorded the man who remains arguably the greatest poet of the French language.

VIII

ROMANTICISM was out of fashion in the 1880s. The cynicism and dislocation we associate with so much of twentieth-century art were already affecting man's outlook as the nineteenth century drew to a close. Small wonder Hugo's broad-based and positive achievement was belittled in the decades after his death but it is worth remembering the high esteem with which, among others, Baudelaire, Leconte de Lisle, Proust, Valéry and Aragon have regarded his work. On this side of the Channel men like Tennyson and Swinburne also showed their profound respect for Hugo. To the former he was:

Victor in Drama, Victor in Romance,
Cloud-weaver of phantasmal hopes and fears,
French of the French, and Lord of human tears;
Child-lover; Bard whose fame-lit laurels glance
Darkening the wreaths of all that would advance,
Beyond our strait, their claim to be thy peers.

Swinburne addressed him as one 'nursed in airs apart' and added:

Thou art chief of us, and lord;
Thy song is as a sword
Keen-edged and scented in the blade from flowers.

He is, finally, incomparable. If he can be classed within a French tradition at all it is that of Rabelais, Balzac and Proust himself, the tradition of daring all to come to terms with all. He has flaws as they have. But above all he is not afraid of the contradictions inherent in life itself, not afraid of imperfections, nor of failure.

Hugo is a linear poet. That is to say he achieves his effects by the accumulation of cross-references moving on the same plane. These continue to inform each other so that the lyrical awareness (which most people have) is raised to the pitch of great poetry which could be defined as an inspired organization of the relevant. Hugo had also what many other great poets have lacked – the light touch. Conscious of his prophetic rôle he could thunder apocalyptic truths but in poem after poem, with the casualness that hides art, he produced the most delicate effects: 'Mes deux filles', a single sentence, catches an evanescent moment of youth and grace. In 'Unité' a charming epigram is given the most subtle parallels of colour and place as the sun, poised at evening above the rim of the earth, matches in the east a daisy hanging above a wall. In the poem describing the pilgrimage he is to make to his daughter's grave, 'Demain, dès l'aube . . .' the easiest of colloquial expressions are lent a haunting poignancy by their juxtaposition with more 'literary' effects.

He was a master craftsman, at home in a multiplicity of

verse-forms. The variety of his inventiveness is astonishing. He could control, with ease, rhymed two-syllable lines and, before Verlaine advocated its use, wrote many poems in deliberately 'uneven' metre. He once as a *tour de force* wrote a couplet in which every syllable is rhymed:

> Gal, amant de la reine, alla, tour magnanime,
> Galamment de l'arène à la Tour Magne à Nîmes.

As for other great poets his natural language was poetry which he spoke as easily as water issues from a source. To use Barbey d'Aurevilly's analogy he shows 'the absolute sovereignty of the instrumentalist over his instrument, the exact point where the player and the instrument become one.' It was one of his virtues that he believed the act of poetry was so important that it should embrace every aspect of human affairs, that poetry was not a marginal but a central activity and that any poet worth his salt should accept all the rôles of mind, emotion, senses and the soul without flinching, without fearing either the shouts of those who demand public poetry or the murmurs of those who are engaged in the building of ivory towers. To be a poet, pure, simple, impure, complex – that was Hugo's rôle.

'None of us has the honour of having a life that is his alone. My life is yours, your life is mine, you live what I live; destiny is one. Then take this mirror and look at yourself in it. People complain sometimes because a writer says "I". "Speak to us of ourselves," they cry. Alas, when I speak to you of myself I am speaking of you.' With these words Hugo introduced *Les Contemplations*. The 'I' is Hugo but it stands for man.

IX

MY AIM IN presenting these translations has been primarily to share with other readers a poet I have admired all my adult life. Poems have been selected from all periods in his long and distinguished career and if, out of sixty-six poems, twenty-three come from *Les Contemplations* that is partly because it is one of the very great collections of French poetry but also because most of the poems in *La Légende des siècles*, his other major work, are so long that to include them would be to preclude examples of his genius from other books.

The translations are as accurate as I can make them. That is to say they are not word-for-word. It would not, I hope, be possible to use this book as a crib. The aim has been a re-creation of the poetic effect in English and this has meant – inevitably – altering word-order and moving sentences about. As far as possible I have incorporated any necessary explanations inside the texts themselves but where extra details might be of assistance there are notes at the back of the book.

Each poem has been translated on its own terms in an attempt to find a form appropriate to it in English. In 'Oceano nox' I have tried to indicate the way Hugo displaced the traditionally regular caesura so as to gain a special dramatic effect. Some of the versions are metrical, others syllabic, others – the longer poems in particular – in varying rhythm. In 'Attente' the sense of rhyme seemed more important than arboreal verisimilitude and therefore *chêne* (oak) has become *pine*. In 'Après la bataille' a monosyllable would not fit the metre and so I 'translated' *rhum* as *brandy*. I hope these two instances are forgivable – and that there are no other howlers.

There is no content in a poem without form. Poetry is also a different language from prose. *Winter*, in prose, is a time of year. In the line

How like a winter hath my absence been

apparently the same word has overtones of sterility and loss, of lack of fruitfulness and cold despair; and yet because there is a cycle of the seasons, Shakespeare can imply an eventual return to the warmth of love in that the presence of winter implies the coming of spring. Cocteau referred to poetry as a language apart which poets can use without fear of being overheard since nations are accustomed to taking it as merely a certain way of using their own. It seems to me therefore that to put the original poem into English prose is a valueless exercise – trying to establish 'meaning' while jettisoning all attempt (however inadequate) to make the experience of equivalent force. The English version must lag well behind the French poem – no translation can be more than a two-dimensional shadow of the creations and discoveries of the original – but it ought at least to persuade readers that an act of the poetic imagination is being dealt with, not an act of prose. The language used and the techniques adopted should – ideally – satisfy their expectations that the text before them echoes, imitates, in some poor way matches the soaring and unknown qualities of the original – the piano-transcription of an orchestral score or our earth-bound nightingale and not the real song sung in a platonic heaven.

Conversely it is, I think, important not to invent, embroider or drag in what does not belong to the poem in a misguided attempt to soup up the translation. This would lay as opaque a covering over the true poem as a prose-reduction. The text of the original must be the finishing-point as well as the starting-point. The exigencies of one's own language introduce new tensions and new harmonies but the tone of the original must be aimed for absolutely.

It is of course impossible for a modern translator to get inside the skin of a nineteenth-century sensibility – and surely undesirable to attempt pastiche, to mimic the language of, say, Arnold or Beddoes. One cannot ignore the fact that one is writing in 1978, nor that the language accepted by poets alters subtly decade by decade. This is why translations need to be redone every generation or so, for the qualities one sees so readily in poems of the past in one's own language are rarely perceived through the medium of an outdated translation. Or rather the conventions one accepts – indeed relishes – with historical imagination become a positive hindrance when trying to hear through translation the reverberations the original poet would communicate to a reader in his own language today. Even so there is a 'brake' on a translator's sensibility – he cannot haul a nineteenth-century poet into a world he never knew. There is room here for an element of respect, a slight distancing. So, while eliminating archaisms, one has I think to steer clear of a frantically modish idiom that would in fact date before the ink dries on the page.

Hugo is a major poet. In his attention to detail, in his visionary sweep, in his passionate hurling of questions at the stars and in his tranquil celebration of the status quo he is uniquely tender and uniquely grand. If some of his great qualities have crept through the fence of my translations I shall be well pleased.

HARRY GUEST
Exeter, 1978

The Distance, The Shadows

In the Valley of Cherizy

Factus sum peregrinus . . . et quaesivi qui simul
contristaretur, et non fuit.   Ps. LXVIII

Perfice gressus meos semitis tuis.   Ps. XVI

I am become . . . an alien . . . and I looked for
some to take pity, but there was none. Ps. 69, A.V.
Hold up my goings in thy paths, that my
footsteps slip not.   Ps. 17, A.V.

A wanderer sits down among the still
shadows of a valley in whose beauty
    saddened, alone, he contemplates
one bird fleeing from another,
    a snake marring the pond
    and a bulrush moved by the wind.

Man also flees from man.
And often misfortune slithers across a young
    heart however noble or pure.
Happy the humble reed which the sudden
        storm raging past
    breaks when it is still in its flower.

The wanderer implores that storm.
Fatigued already with the course, he's far
    yet from the finish of his pain.
Alone, unaided, he sees stretching out
mist-blurred beneath an ominous sunrise
    the great wilderness of the future.

His life will drag on from disgust
to disgust. What profit is there in false
    treasures envied by a false pride?
He seeks a loyal heart, companion in grief,
        in vain. No aid
    will smooth his way, no others laugh
        when he's joyful,
    and none will weep to join him in his tears.

His fate is to be forlorn,
a life of isolation like the grim
cypress growing in the valley
far from the virgin lily that discloses
her bud to the day – no loving vine
sends a green tendril to embrace
its black boughs bringing charm into its shade.

The wanderer has taken brief
refuge here before attempting the hill.
Silence at least answers to his distress.
In crowds he is alone but here his sweet
companion is solitude.

Let these trees, these glades, gay sanctuaries, lonely
like him although unlike him calm,
protect the unhappy wanderer from the eyes
of men and let the stream
wash from his feet the mire of their cities
and the dust of their roads.

Consoled among these shadows let him sing
the long ideal dream of our most sombre days –
a girl both pure and beautiful,
smiling, unwed –
and if he is refused her living hand
let him imagine their immortal souls
eternally together in the grave.

This world does not enslave his mind.
Hope lifts him free of bitter memories.
Two shadows now
will dominate his life, one in the past
and one in the future.

What angel will lead the charming
consoler towards him? When will the star
of friendship shine like a new sun
over his orphaned days?

He will not forfeit unforgotten
virtues to gain the prize.
Letting the reed bend to the wind's caprice
he'll be the oak before the storm
to break sooner than yield.

Feeling no fear, he sees the storm approach.
Farewell then to the stream
that lulled him among the thickets.
Farewell to the fair valley where he found
an echo to his lament and farewell
to these fortunate woods where one
may grieve in peace.

Happy the man deep in some lonely valley
who lives and dies in the paternal fields
knowing nothing of the world,
seeing nothing but the sky.

July 1821

Morning

Moriturus morituræ!

The veils of morning open on the hills.
Increasing light now whitens the old tower.
And glory blends with joy –
    the first birds singing in the wood
    match the first fires of day.

Smile at the radiance the sky puts on.
For tomorrow if the coffin grasps me
    you'll see as brilliant a sun
        shine on your eyes in tears
and the same birds will celebrate the dawn
    above my black and silent grave.

But the soul wakes
ravished before another skyline where
    endless the future is unfurled.
At daybreak in eternity
    you wake from life as from
a sombre night or a disturbing dream.

April 1822

The Boy

O horror! horror! horror! – SHAKESPEARE, *Macbeth*

The Turks were here. Ruin. Grief.
Chios, island of vines,
now a charred reef –
Chios, once shaded with blossom,
Chios, whose tides advancing
mirrored great woods, slopes, palaces,
sometimes at dusk a chorus
of young girls dancing.

All is deserted. Save
near blackened walls where
one blue-eyed child, a Greek boy, sits
head bowed in shame. He has
for shelter, for support one
hawthorn, white-flowering,
like him in the havoc forgotten.

Barefoot on harsh rock,
poor child, to free from tears
those sky-coloured eyes, sea-blue,
stormy with weeping
what can I give to make you
lift your blond head and let delight
flash across your glance?

Your fine hair never yet
insulted by any blade trails
like dishevelled leaves of a willow
over your fair brow grieving.
What can I give to make you
toss back your head in joy
sending the bright hair curling
once again over your shoulders?

What could scatter
the misery clouding your gaze –

that lily, blue like your eyes, that grows
by a dark well in distant Persia?
that fruit that hangs in Paradise
high on a tree so huge
a galloping horse takes a hundred years
escaping from its shade?

Will you smile again if I give you
a fair bird of the forests
singing more sweetly than the flute
more gaily than the cymbals?
What can I give you – flower, sleek fruit,
wondrous bird? The child then,
the Greek boy with blue eyes, said, 'Friend,
'give me some powder and some shot.'

June 1828

Waiting

Esperaba, desperada.

Squirrel, go and climb the pine,
reach that branch beneath the cloud
thinner than a length of twine.
Stork that each day haunts the proud
steeple, wing towards the keep,
leave your tower for the bell
on the topmost citadel.

Eagle, leave your eyrie, fly
to the age-old mountain peak
where eternal winters lie.
Let the early lark whose beak
scatters song as dawn appears
leave the ground and soaring high
mount the summits of the sky.

From the treetop, from the spire
on the watch-tower, can you see –
from the mountain, from the air
red with sunrise, can you see
through the haze a tossing plume,
then a smoking horse and then
my beloved once again?

June 1828

Reverie

Lo giorno se n'andava, e l'aer bruno
Toglieva gli animai che sono'n terra
Dalle fatiche loro.

DANTE

Leave me to myself. The horizon smokes,
conceals its outline with a turn of mist.
The sun is reddening to disappear.
The only gold along the slope
is on great autumn beeches where
the woods have rusted in the light and rain.

If only now – while I alone
dream by the window and the shadows
gather behind me down the corridor –
if only now some Moorish town would rise,
spread on the skyline like an outburst flare
and rip the fog with pinnacles of gold!

I need such splendour for my songs which are
as sombre otherwise as late year clouds.
Such sorcery reflected in my gaze would leave –
its distant business one gradual fade –
the thousand turrets of its faery palaces
to linger jagged on the darkened sky.

September 1828

34

Sunset

The sun has set this evening in clouds –
a storm tomorrow, evening, then the dark:
then dawn again, its candour streaked with haze,
then nights, then days, prints left by fleeing time.

These days must pass, pass crowding on
expanse of sea and mountain-top,
on glittering rivers, woods that shift with blurred
murmurs like psalms from loved mouths of the dead.

Stretches of ocean, of sheer upland rock –
wrinkled, unaging – pass restored through time,
and the woods green and again green. The river
takes from the hills the stream it feeds the sea.

But I, bent lower underneath each dawn,
pass by, and chilled in all this gaiety of sun
must soon depart, this splendour all around,
leaving no gap in the world's wide radiance.

22 April 1829

To a Traveller

One part of the world has no idea how the other lives and governs itself – PHILIPPE DE COMMINES

You've returned, my friend, from one of those long
journeys which age us so fast we exchange
     youth for early wisdom.
You've cut the surface of every ocean
and you would put a girdle round the earth
     with the wake of your ship.

The suns of twenty skies have ripened you
and wherever your wavering desires
     have led you to discard
and gather, like farmers reaping, sowing,
you've picked up something and have also left
     something there of yourself.

While I, your friend, less fortunate, less wise,
watched the changeless passage of the seasons
     against the same skyline –
like the green tree that stands as a landmark
shedding its days by our threshold I took
     root here where my house is.

You've seen so many people you're fatigued
and, tired by what men are, return at last
     to take your rest in God.
You've told me sadly of pointless journeys
and from your boots the dust of three worlds fell
     by the ash of my fire.

Now that your heart's replete with grave matters,
hands placed on the blond heads of my children,
     you show friendship when you
enquire – though the answer's bitter to find –
about my father, mother, eldest boy.
     They're on a voyage too,

though travelling beneath no sun or moon
and they may take nothing along with them
  so strict is the captain.
Their voyage is serious and has no end –
it happens slowly among grim faces,
  one we'll all have to take.

As when you left I watched their departure.
At different times, one after the other,
  the three of them set off.
I loved them yet one day I had to put
them in the earth. Like any miser I
  buried my treasure deep.

I saw them leave. Fearful, powerless, I saw
three times emblems of mourning decorate
  that corridor with black.
I wept like a girl over their cold hands
but after the coffin was shut I saw
  their souls open gold wings.

I saw them leave soaring like three swallows
searching far off for a more certain spring,
  for a fairer summer.
My mother was the first. She saw heaven
and in her dying eyes there was a light
  one glimpses nowhere else.

And then my first-born followed her. And then
my father worn by forty years of war,
  a veteran and proud.
Now they are gone. All three sleep in the shade
while their spirits are on that dark journey
  going where we'll all go.

Tonight when the moon is waning let us
climb the hill together and see the place
  where our ancestors lie.
When we are there I'll show you the dead town

that lies near the town asleep and ask you
    which sleeps the better now.

Come: we'll lie down in silence on the ground
while Paris quiets the bustle of its day
    and listen to the dead,
the countless harvest of the son of man,
murmuring softly in their sepulchres
    like seeds in a furrow.

How many people live in joy who should
still be weeping over those they have lost,
    brothers, sisters! The dead
last a short time. Leave them beneath the stone.
In the coffin they crumble to dust less
    quickly than in our hearts.

You've travelled far. Who can explain the power
years have to conquer grief? How many dead
    do we forget each hour?
Who can tell how each sorrow is blunted,
who can tell how many graves are effaced
    by one day's growth of grass?

6 July 1829

The Child Appears

The rafters ring with joy – ANDRÉ CHÉNIER

The child appears. All present
clap their hands. Its glance
has radiance causing radiance
in other eyes.
Brows scored with grief
or lined perhaps with sin
grow smooth when the child appears,
guiltless and joyful.

Whether the threshold's green with June
or winter has
huddled the chairs together
flickering in firelight –
the child comes in and joy
will shine among us. We laugh,
call out. Watching it start to
walk the mother
trembles.

We'll stir the fire sometimes
and talk of politics or God,
of poetry and the way the soul
lifts in prayer.
Enter the child. No more
of nation, paradise or hallowed verse.
Grave talk
pauses to smile.

In darkness, the time
for sleep, for dreaming, at an hour
when water whispers among reeds
as though lamenting – dawn
suddenly a distant glow
causes birdsong and churchbells.

A child is daybreak. I'm the fields
turning to flowers whenever dawn
breathes over them.
I am dark branches in a wood where
the child alone
brings the first golden
stirrings of the day.

Your eyes, my child, have all
the candour of eternity –
your hands perform
no evil and your steps
have not yet trespassed in our mire –
your blond hair makes
a halo for
an angel's head.

You come among us like the dove
that sped towards the Ark
on wings of sky –
your feet too light, too tender yet
to try the ground.
You see
but do not understand our world:
dual purity – a soul
unspoiled, a body virginal.

A child is lovely with its smile,
good faith, a voice
searching for words
and tears soon dried.
Its gaze
goes everywhere and is entranced –
an astonished heart offered to life,
a mouth eager for kisses.

Lord, may I, may those I love –
my brothers, cousins, friends –

even my enemies
triumphant in their wrong –
never see a summer
without scarlet flowers,
never see a cage
without a singing bird,
never see a hive
without honey-bees,
never see a house
without children.

18 May 1830

'Whoever you may be . . .'

Quien no ama, no vive.

Whoever you may be – young, old, rich, wise –
    if you have never waited while
she through the twilight with a step that dies
away in music passes veiled in white
    leaving along your heart a trail
of radiance like a meteor's on the night;

If all you know of love is what you're told
    the poets sing in their delight
and sighing sing about those hours of gold
when they possess one heart where nothing lies
    concealed and need no other light,
no stars, no suns, except one pair of eyes;

And if you've never lingered in despair
    under bright windows where some ball
is glittering in splendour till the hour
at last arrives when through the opened door,
    flushed, blue-eyed, young and beautiful,
the loved one comes with garlands in her hair;

And if you've never known how it can hurt
    when that soft hand you so desire
is chosen by another and her heart
beats on another's – if you've never burned
    with jealous rage at watching her
waltz while the petals drift from her garland;

And if you've never run downhill ablaze
    with passion shouting like a god –
if you have never sat beneath lime-trees
at evening while the countless stars shine down,
    breathing with her the sweet cool shade
and speaking in low voices though alone;

And if no hand has ever made your hand
    tremble – if one phrase said in turn
'I love you' has not made the day expand
in joy – if you don't pity every king
    who sought a sceptre or a crown
though he already knew what love could bring;

At night when the last candle flickers lower,
    when mist steals round and buries all
the pointed steeples and each lofty tower,
Paris, too tired to count them, lets the black
    hours sow vain longings as they fall
twelve times from belfries scattered in the dark;

If you have never (while the world's asleep
    and she lies dreaming far away
forgetful of you) wept as children weep
and spent the whole night calling out her name
    hoping she'd come with one more cry
and wished for death and cursed your mother's womb;

If you have never felt a woman's eye
    awake in you a different soul,
another heaven, so you'd gladly die
upon the rack for her though her disdain
    makes playthings of your tears, then you'll
have never loved nor ever suffered pain.

November 1831

Tomorrow

Tomorrow is the great affair.
What can tomorrow's dawn expect?
Today man sows the cause somewhere,
Tomorrow God brings the effect –
A flash of lightning in the sail,
A cloud that covers up the Pole,
A traitor casting off the veil,
The siege that batters at the realm,
A star that tumbles from its zone
Or Paris after Babylon.
Today the velvet's on the throne –
Tomorrow just the planks of elm.

August 1832

from NAPOLÉON II, *part 2*

Concerning the Ball at the Hôtel de Ville

So lights are lit high on the Hôtel de Ville.
The prince glitters with gold medals, and torches
will gleam among the gables this evening
like bright inspiration on a poet's brow!
This feast, though, friends, is not the light of thought.
It's not a rich banquet France requires pressingly,
it's not a dance that's urgently desired
by the mass of miseries we call a city.

The powerful should prefer to tend some wound
that worries all our wise philosophers –
prop up the lower stairs that lead on high,
enlarge the work-room and reduce the scaffold,
care for each child who dwells without bread in the dark,
create a paradise for the blasphemous poor,
rather than burn a thousand candles to keep
a few fools awake all night around a little noise.

You wives who rule beneath our roofs, chaste, devout,
like flowers yielding fragrance in our houses –
you have been lucky so your lives are virtuous,
you've never needed to struggle against evil
and hunger's insidious poison has never
said, 'Sell me your body' and that means your soul.
Your hearts are full of innocence and fresh joy,
your modesty is wrapped in more pure linen
than ever the image of Isis, the veiled goddess.
This dance for you is one whole dawn of stars –
you run to it smiling while there's suffering elsewhere.
Your loveliness has never learned about misery,
fortune has fitted you for the highest sphere,
you live glittering in brightness and because your gaze
is dazzled with light you never look
at what's crushed underfoot in the dark far below you.

This is what happens: the prince and the wealthy
attempt to enthral you though you have everything.

You have beauty from birth and are decked out with jewels.
Intoxicated by the hum that you hear,
like a silken moth towards the flame, you fly
to the open door that pours light over the pavement.
You set off for the dance and never dream
that among the people passing where you pass,
crowding amazed at the carriage and livery,
are other women no less well-adorned than you,
made up and set for sale at each street-corner –
ghosts who still bleed in the gap where love should be.
Their fair shoulders bare as yours are for the ball,
they've come here on purpose to watch you pass,
concealing their grim mourning with mockery,
flowers in their hair, mud on their feet, hate in their hearts.

May 1832

'Dawn is igniting . . .

Dawn is igniting,
dense shades scud away;
dreaming, like mist,
departs with the night;
eyelids and blossoms
tremble apart;
everywhere sounds are
making a start.

Song now or murmur –
speaking at once
smoke and the foliage,
bird's nest and thatch;
wind in the oak-tree,
drops from the source,
what was a breath moves
into a voice.

New life is returning –
the hearth picks up flame,
the baby its rattle,
the fiddle its bow;
passion and madness
under the sun
take up once more what
they had begun.

Thinker or lover
endlessly moved,
flying again for
one ultimate goal:
the skiff to its mooring,
the compass to north,
the bee to a willow
and I to the truth.

December 1834

'Since I have placed my lip . . .'

Since I have placed my lip
to your still brimming cup,
Since my pale brow has leaned
into your sheltering hand,
Since I at times have caught
the hidden fragrance of your heart –

Since I have heard you say
words of love's mystery,
Since I have known your kiss
smile upon mine and press
against my own and seen
your eyes in tears mirroring mine –

Since one ray from your star
so often veiled too far
from me has shone across
the gap that severs us,
Since you have let me seize
one rose-leaf of your sweeter days –

I can tell the swift years,
'Pass by. Pass with your cares.
'I will not age. Take all
'your withered flowers that fall
'and go. Within my soul
'there is a flower none can steal.

'Let time's wing brush the jar
'I've filled to the brim nor
'spill one drop. I've more flame
'in my heart now than time
'has ash and I possess
'more love than time forgetfulness.'

1 January 1835   12:30 a.m.

To Albrecht Dürer

Old forests and the thick sap flowing
        from the black shafts
of the alders to the white birch-trunks –
        here, many times,
pale, scared, hurrying across the glade,
        never risking
a glance behind him, Albrecht Dürer,
        my master, used
to go trembling and I stand here now
        awe-struck before
the black thickets in these pictures where
        his tranced eye saw
distinctly, overgrown with shadows,
        the faun with webbed
fingers, the wood-demon with green eyes,
        Pan wreathing flowers
round the cave where the great painter sits
        meditating
and the dryad, her hands filled with leaves.

        For the forest
is for him a place without order
        where what is dream
what is real become mingled. Pine-trees
        lean there brooding
and the twisted branches of elms make
        a thousand shapes,
the wind stirs their darkness, nothing seems
        entirely dead
entirely alive, the water flees,
        the brooklime sips,
on the slope ash-trees slowly pull back
        their gnarled black roots
from the bristling tide of undergrowth
        whose brambles are
stealing towards them. The swan-necked flowers
        bend over pools

to find a mirror and the artist
in passing by
awakes strange monsters with scaly throats
who squeeze the huge
knots of the trees between their fingers
and look at him
with luminous eyes from a dark cave –
what are they? strength
of nature, spirit of the plants, soul
in matter – all
covered with coarse skin or living bark.

Neither, master,
can I wander through the woods without
feeling my heart
pierced with awe seeing the grass shiver
and blurred symbols
hanging on branches swayed by the wind.
God bears witness
to the mystery behind facts and knows
the way in wild
places, burning with secrets, I've seen
immense living
oak-trees quivering with souls like my own
and laughing and
murmuring together in the shade.

20 April 1837

My Thoughts

My thoughts?
        Far from the roof
sheltering you, my thoughts
are of you, my children, and the hopes
that lie in you. My summer days
have ripened and the sun
has started its decline. Each year
the shadow of your branches
creeps further up my wall
yet some furled petals still retain
the secret dazzle of your dawn.

I think of the two younger ones
laughing as they cry.
The threshold must be green
where they babble mingling
games with quarrels both with charm –
two flowers occasionally
rub against each other as they sway.

All fathers worry and I think
about the two older ones
already further from the shore
among deeper waves. They lean
their heads to one side now, the boy
all curiosity, the girl all thought.

Alone here, sad, I think these things
while sailors sing beneath the cliff.
The sea at evening
seems to breathe and sigh
when waves advance, recede.
The wind blends salt into the air
that stirs with strange
echoes of land and water.

I think of you, my children, seeing
a table surrounded with laughter,
a fireplace crackling,
all the piety and care
your mother and her father shed
in tenderness.
Here at my feet the clear sea spreads
set with sails and mirroring the stars.
Boatmen casually
glance from the unending
sea to the unending
sky and I think of you, my children,
trying to sound
the depth of love I have for you,
its gentleness, its power –
and in comparison how small the sea!

15 July 1837
by the sea at Fécamp

Night on the Ocean

Saint-Valery-sur-Somme

Captains seamen how many
leaving light-hearted on distant cruises
vanished beyond the bleak horizon
how many have gone confronting their fate
one fathomless sea one moonless night
buried for ever beneath a blind ocean

How many masters dead with their crew
one storm ripped all the pages from their life
its blast dispersing them over the waves
who can tell their end sunk in the depths
each passing wave loaded with plunder
one seized the longboat one the sailors

Who knows your fate poor drowned skulls
that roll through dark expanses of the sea
to knock bone brows on nameless reefs
how many parents one dream left
died expecting each day on the shore
  you who did not return

Talking about you sometimes at sunset
light-hearted groups on the rusty anchors
include your names shrouded in shadow
among laughter songs tales of adventure
and kisses filched from your fiancées
while the green seaweed covers you sleeping

They ask if you're kings on distant islands
abandoning home for a more fertile shore
and then all mention of you stops forgotten
corpse lost in water name sunk in memory
time casting shade again on shade
spreads on the dark sea dark oblivion

And soon your shade   is vanished from view
one has his ship to care for   one his plough
only   when storms rage vanquishing the night
your pale-browed widows   weary of waiting
speak of you still   stirring the embers
     left on the grate   left in their hearts

The grave at last   closes their eyelids
and nothing now recalls your name   no stone
in the narrow churchyard   answering in echoes
not one willow   shedding dead leaves
not one ballad   simple repeated
sung by a beggar   near the old bridge

Where now   those seamen sunk in black night
waves   how many dismal tales you know
deep waves   feared by mothers at prayer
your tales are whispered   as the tide sweeps in
and this is why the sea   has a despairing sound
at evening when we hear   waves approach the shore!

July 1836

June Nights

In summer, after the day's passed, spread
with flowers the meadows shed
a fragrance masking the sense. Sleep
becomes transparent and you keep
your eyes closed half aware
of the drifting sounds of summer.

Stars are purer now
and the shadows show
themselves less dark. Half-light
is hazed gently across the full height
of the sky. Dawn bides its time seeming
to hover on the horizon all night long.

28 September 1837

Olympio: His Sadness

No fields were black nor was the sky
       dismal, the day
blazed limitless and blue over the earth,
the air was fragrant, sanctified, the green
      meadows shone as he saw
        once again
    the places where through many wounds
      his heart's blood had been spilled.

The autumn smiled its welcome, slopes
      fleeced with forest
were hardly touched with yellow though the sky
showed gold. The birds turning their flight upwards
      in praise of the maker
        named by all
    told Him perhaps in their songs what
      they had learned of mankind.

He wanted to see everything
      again, the pool
by the clear spring, the poor man's hovel where
they'd emptied their purses, the bent ash-tree,
      the hidden places deep
        in the wood,
    trees under which they'd kissed and lost
      themselves inside their love.

He sought the garden with the house
      set by itself,
the iron gate showing the path that slanted
between the orchard banks. He was alone
      and pale and every tree
        that he passed
    showed him the shades of sadness cast
      by days that are no more.

He heard a wind go shivering through
       the wood he loves,
a sweet wind finding a response that sighs
in us, wakes tremulous thoughts of love and stirs
       the oak or sways the rose,
         a wind that
   seems to express all things and one
       by one touches them all.

Leaves lay strewn in the solitude
       of the forest –
as he passed by they lifted in the still
air, scurried behind his steps and entered
       the garden – thus, when sad,
        our thoughts rise
   for a moment on their hurt wings,
       one moment, then fall back.

In silence, contemplating long
       the hallowed shapes
of nature, all the peaceful fields that spread
towards the distance, he dreamed till evening.
       In the narrow valley
        he looked now
   at the sky now at its image
       reflected in the lake.

Remembering what had occurred,
       all the delight,
he wandered sadly all day long and looked,
without going in, over the closed fence.
       When night came, his heart dark
        as the grave
   showed him what he was, an outcast,
       and then he cried aloud:

'I've come to learn what sorrow has to teach,
        returning here to see
if anything remains of those far days
    and if this happy valley's kept or lost
    all that I left here of my heart.

'A short time is enough to alter all.
        Nature, serenely calm,
is able to forget and ceaselessly
adapting breaks the secret threads which bound
    our dearest memories to our hearts.

'Familiar clearings of the past are changed,
        the bowers overgrown,
the trees we carved our names on have blown down,
our roses have been trampled by children
        jumping the ditch beside the road.

'A wall's been built around the little spring
        where on hot days she'd drink
on strolls through the wood, a dryad, half shade,
half light, then, her hand cupped, let the water
    run through her fingers like bright pearls.

'They've also paved the rough uneven track
        where displayed so clearly
in the sand her delicate footprint showed
the contrast between its charming smallness
        and the heavier marks of my stride.

'The venerable milestone where she liked
        in those far days to sit
and wait for me is chipped and broken now
by the carts jolting it in the evening
        as they creak along the dark road.

'Here the forest's been thinned out and here fresh
        trees are being planted –
there's almost nothing left alive that once
went with our love, the memory's dispersed,
        cold ashes taken by the wind.

'We might not have existed, you and I.
        We had our day and our
superfluous cries can never bring it back.
I weep and the air plays with the bough, my
        house looks on me as a stranger.

'Others will pass where you and I once passed.
        We came here, others now
will come and take up the unending dream
which we began to shape and which they too
        will be unable to complete.

'For on this earth nothing is ended, no
        human achieves his task –
neither the best nor worst. We all wake up
at the same moment in the dream – what starts
        in this world finishes elsewhere.

'Yes, other couples in their turn coming
        in innocence to this
enchanted sanctuary will draw grave
reveries of nature that go with a love
        hidden away in happiness.

'Others will have our fields, our secret paths.
        Your wood, my darling, now
belongs to strangers. Different women
thoughtlessly will come along disturbing
        the water where your bare feet bathed.

'We loved each other here in vain. Nothing
            remains that's ours on these
flowered hills where our two passions were dissolved
into one. By now impassive nature
        has taken back all she once gave.

'And will, I wonder, these ravines, these cool
            streams, arbours of ripe fruit,
boughs with their nests, these grottoes, copses, glades,
will they murmur secrets to newcomers
        and sing to others songs we know?

'We understood so well all that they had
            to say, echoing back
each mood, attentive or austere, trying
to catch the depth of what was whispered here
        but not disturb the mystery.

'I call upon this valley to reply,
            on the forms of nature
sheltering here in this fine wilderness:
When she and I are both inside our graves
        lying full length as if asleep,

'Can you be so unfeeling as to know
            we are both stretched there dead,
dead with our thoughts of love perished as well,
and still continue with your smiles of joy,
        your songs, your peaceful festival?

'Will you, sensing us wander through your woods,
            pale phantoms, recognized
by path and hillside, not whisper to us
the kind of secrets that are shared by friends
        meeting after a long absence?

'Could you observe our shades pass where our steps
        once firmly trod and not
feel some sadness watching as her wan ghost
tugs at my hand and leads me to some spring
    trickling mournfully through the grass?

'And if somewhere, far in the shadows, where
        no one can overlook,
the flowers are sheltering two lovers lost
in rapture, could you not breathe in their ear:
    "You are alive. Think of the dead."?

'God lends us for a brief time the meadows,
        the fountains, the great woods
shivering with summer, the secret rocks,
the lakes, the plains, the rich blue sky, where we
    invest so many dreams of love

'and then He takes them from us. One dark gust
        extinguishes our flame.
He shrouds in night places we helped to shine
with love, tells the valley to blur all trace
    of us, even forget our names.

'Then let the house and the shadowed garden
        forget us, let the grass
split the threshold and the bramble conceal
our footprints, birds sing, streams flow, leaves uncurl –
    we remember though they forget,

'because they are the shade where lovers can
        find rest and cool water
to slake their thirst. This valley was a last
refuge where we took comfort, hand in hand,
    and shedding tears shared our sorrow.

'With age all passions move away – one takes
    the mask, one the dagger,
like a group of travelling players singing
as they go and dwindling until one by
    one they vanish over the hill.

'But nothing can efface the charm of love,
    its torch gleams through the fog,
when young you curse the blaze in your hand, when
old you bless its glow – captured by the joys
    of love as well as its sorrows.

'And when at last the head is bent low, weighed
    by the years, and man lives
without a plan or aim or vision, feels
he is no more than a ruined graveyard
    where virtues and illusions rot –

'When, pondering, man turns into himself,
    feeling the ice approach
his heart, and counts, the way you'd count the dead
on a field of battle, every fallen
    sorrow, every extinguished dream –

'Like someone searching lamp in hand, he goes
    far from real things, far from
the laughter of the world, and slowly starts
down a dark staircase, down to the empty
    place that lies beyond the last step –

'There in that darkness lit by no star's gleam,
    there in the innermost
night where life appears to have reached its end –
something still stirs beneath a veil – sacred
    memory asleep in the shadow.'

21 October 1837

The Song of Those Who Go to Sea

BRETON TUNE

Farewell to the land
The waves start to swell
Farewell to the land
Farewell
Blue is the sky and blue the swell
Farewell

Next to the house the vine grows tall
The flowers show gold above the wall

Goodbye to the land
The wood, fields and sky
Goodbye to the land
Goodbye

Goodbye to the girl who wears your ring
The sky is black, the salt winds sting

Farewell to the land
To the girls you knew well
Farewell to the land
Farewell
Blue was the sky and blue the swell
Farewell

Grief for the future dims our eye
The dark sea leads to a darker sky

I'll pray for that land
With all my heart
Loving it well
As I depart
Farewell to the land
Farewell

at sea, 1 August 1852

The Huntsman of the Night

'Who are you, stranger? Flocks of crows
'Wing through the wood. A dark wind blows
    'And it will rain tonight.'
'I am the one each shadow knows –
    'The huntsman of the night.'

The forest leaves are stirring as the gale
    Approaches – soon
The witches gathering will start to wail
    Their sabbath tune.
High in a gap among the clouds now, pale
    There shines the moon.

    Hunt down the many-antlered deer
    Coursing through wood and field in fear.
        Put the Czar's men to flight.
    Hunt down the enemy – evening's here,
        O huntsman of the night.

The forest leaves . . .

    Make the horn set woods echoing.
    Get the hounds ready now and bring
        Power to set evil right.
    Hunt down the bishop, hunt the king,
        O huntsman of the night.

The forest leaves . . .

    Thunder and lightning cross the sky.
    All shelter's gone, the fox must fly,
        Hope's fallen from the height.
    Hunt down the judge and hunt the spy,
        O huntsman of the night.

The forest leaves . . .

Demons from hell are prancing drunk
With blood around the rotten trunk –
    Your courage still stays bright.
Hunt down the priest and hunt the monk,
    O huntsman of the night.

The forest leaves . . .

Hunt the grim boar down. Fetch the rope.
No wild beast need feel any hope.
    Duty's become delight.
Hunt down the emperor, hunt the pope,
    O huntsman of the night.

The forest leaves . . .

But now one wolf has taken heart.
Time for our fiercest dogs to start
    Jaws open for the bite –
Hunt down the brigand Bonaparte,
    O huntsman of the night.

The tempest raging through the wood has ceased.
    Leaves fall like tears.
The sorcerers have left their deadly feast.
    The listener hears
The lucid sound of cock-crow in the east
    And dawn appears.

France has regained her pride, her old
Beauty and strength and grace unfold.
    You have become a white
Angel arrayed in robes of gold,
    O huntsman of the night.

The tempest raging through the wood has ceased.
Leaves fall like tears.
The sorcerers have left their deadly feast.
The listener hears
The lucid sound of cock-crow in the east
And dawn appears.

Jersey, 22 October 1852

The Retreat from Moscow

Snow.
Their conquest had defeated them.
For the first time the eagle
lowered its head. Dark days.
The emperor came slowly back
and smoke rose in the sky behind him
where Moscow burned.
Snow.
The harsh winter
fell like an avalanche.
One more white plain after the last white plain.
None could distinguish uniforms or flags.
What was the army had become a herd.
None could make out the vanguard or the flanks.
Snow.
The wounded sheltered against the bellies
of dead horses. Buglers, silent,
frozen at their post,
the bivouacs behind them empty,
sat upright in the saddle, white with frost,
stone lips clamped to the brass mouthpiece.
The shot rained down among white flakes.
Each grenadier, surprised at shivering,
walked deep in thought with ice
hanging on his grey moustache.
Snow.
Snow unceasing. The bitter wind
kept blowing. There was no bread
and the men marched barefoot
through unknown places, slipping
on frozen ground.
There were no heroes any more.
They had become a dream
that wandered through the mist,
a file of shadows on a darkened sky.
Nothing stretched round them but vast

solitude, Russia's
silent revenge. Thick snow
fell noiselessly and one huge shroud
enveloped the huge army. Every man
picked out for death
knew that he was alone.
No exit. No escape. The land
was fatal to invaders.
Two enemies – the czar, the north,
the latter worse.
The guns were discarded so that fires
could be made from their carriages.
If men lay down they died.
Confused, dejected, they kept
fleeing in a vast procession till the waste
land swallowed them up.
Sometimes the snow formed ridges
where a whole regiment
had fallen asleep. It was a rout
like Hannibal's, destruction
as when Attila had passed.
Fugitives, wounded, dying,
crushed among waggons and handcarts,
struggled to gain the bridges.
Ten thousand fell asleep, a hundred woke.
Ney, once the commander of an army, fled
and haggled with three
cossacks over his watch.
Each night the challenge, then
the alarm and then attack. The phantom men
picked up their rifles seeing
appalling horsemen hurtle through the dark,
storm-clouds of fierce assailants shrieking
like birds of prey. Throughout these hours
of darkness every night a whole
army was being lost.
The emperor, looking on, stood
like a tree destined for the axe.
The woodcutter had clambered up
waiting the word to strike.

The spectre of revenge began
hacking the branches off the giant oak
one by one and the living tree, spared till now,
shuddered. Officers, footsoldiers
perished in turn. Those who remained
believing in his star accused
destiny of treason.
Surrounding his tent with love they watched
his shadow on the canvas come and go.
He felt a horror in his soul.
Dazed by disaster, unsure
what to believe or disbelieve, the emperor
turned to God. The man of glory
shook. Napoleon understood
some fault begged expiation and, seeing
his legions scattered on the snow, said,
pallid, uneasy, 'Lord of hosts,
is this my punishment?'
And then he heard his name called and a voice
that spoke among the shadows saying, 'No.'

A Recollection of the Night of 4 December 1851

The boy had been shot –
two bullets in the head.
                    The house
was clean and humble
showing all the signs of peace
and honesty. There was a palm cross
placed above a portrait.

The grandmother was there in tears.

We undressed the child in silence.
His white lips were open, the shy
light in his eyes already
blurring over in death. The arms hung loose
begging support.
He had a boxwood top in his pocket.
The wounds were wide enough for a finger.
The blood looked harmless
like blackberry stains along a hedge in autumn.
The skull was split open like a log.
The old woman watched while we took his clothes off
saying, 'How pale he is. Bring the lamp
nearer. Look how his poor hair
sticks to his forehead.' We finished
and she took him on her knees.
The night was ominous. Rifle-shots sounded
in the street. Others were being killed.
Someone said, 'We need a shroud for the child'
and so we opened the great
wardrobe made of walnut and found
a white sheet while the old woman
carried the body over to the hearth
as though to warm
his limbs already stiffening – but what death's
cold hands have touched
cannot be warmed again by man-made fires.
She leaned down, pulled his stockings off

and took the feet of the corpse in her old hands.
'This is more than a heart will take,' she said.
'He wasn't eight years old.
His teachers – oh yes, his teachers –
he was at school, you know, and they
were pleased with him.
If I had a letter to write he'd do it for me.
And so they've started killing children now.
What are they all then? Monsters? He was playing
there this morning by the window
and they've killed him, my little boy,
my darling. He was going down the street
and they shot him. Sir, I tell you
he was a good Christian boy.
He was kind and gentle.
I'm old. It's time for me to go.
Why didn't M. Bonaparte have me killed
not my boy –'
She broke off, the sobs choking her.
And we were all in tears. She added,
'What's to become of me now
here on my own? Tell me that.
He was all that was left to me
of his poor mother.
Why was he killed?
Will one of you tell me?
Why?
He never cheered for the Republic.'
We stood there bare-headed, shivering,
silent before this grief
none could console.

Politics, it seemed, were beyond her.
Our friend, baptized Napoleon in all honesty,
is poor though he's a prince. He's fond
of palaces and a prince should have
horses and servants as well as cash
for his gaming-table, dinner-parties,
bed-linen, packs of hounds.
And at the same time he's preserving

the church, the family, the French way of life.
He'd like to buy Saint-Cloud, a château
thick with roses in summer
where all the mayors and all the prefects
can come and worship him. And this is why
old grandmothers,
their hands, grey hands, shaken by time,
must sew up little boys of seven
in their shrouds.

'Let all the bugles . . .'

Let all the bugles keep on sounding truth!

Joshua walked in thought, head towards heaven.
His people followed circling Jericho.
The angry prophet raised the trumpet, blew.
The first time they went round, the king laughed loud.
The second time, still laughing, he sent word
'Do you think you will overcome my town
with wind?' The third time soldiers marched behind
the trumpeters, the Ark leading the way.
And little children came and spat on it
and blew their horns to ape the trumpet's peal.
The fourth time, showing they defied the Jews,
the women sat on the old battlements
brown now with rust, and span their thread and jeered
and threw stones at the Hebrews, scorning them.
The fifth time all the blind and lame men crawled
on to those walls of darkness where they mocked
the note that echoed black beneath the clouds.
The sixth time, on his granite tower so high
the eagle made his nest there and so strong
the thunderbolt would strike at it in vain,
the king, holding his sides with laughter, cried,
'These Hebrews play their music well.' Around
the joyous king the elders also laughed –
those men who plot at evening in the temple . . .

The seventh time the great walls fell down flat.

My Two Daughters

Twilight now with cool
shadows falling on the day
as two girls, one a swan,
one a dove, sisters, each
beautiful and both content,
sit on the threshold of the garden
in sweetness, at peace, when
above them white carnations –
their slender stalks set in a marble urn –
are taken by the wind,
lean trembling in the shade,
resembling a flight of butterflies
held there for a moment,
motionless,
living,
in rapture.

June 1842

Old Song of my Young Days

I wasn't thinking of Rose
    Rose came to the woods with me
We talked though what we said
    Is lost to memory

I was as cold as marble
    And walked with a mind perplexed
I spoke of flowers and trees
    Her eye seemed to say 'What next?'

The dew was shining like pearls
    Leaves made the glare a veil
I heard a blackbird sing
    And Rose a nightingale

I was a gloomy sixteen
    She twenty, her eyes were clear
The nightingales sang of Rose
    I heard the blackbirds jeer

Rose stretched her arm in the air
    Her body poised with charm
And gathered a high blackberry
    I didn't see her white arm

Over moss as cool as velvet
    The water flowed with ease
All nature dreaming of love
    Slept among silent trees

Rose untying her shoe-lace
    Innocently put
Her toe in the pure water
    I didn't see her bare foot

I didn't know what to say
    I followed her through the high
Trees and she sometimes smiled
    And sometimes gave a sigh

I saw her beauty only
    As we left the silent wood
'You'll understand one day' she said
    And since, I've understood

Paris, June 1831

Childhood

Songs from the child. The mother on her bed
lay dying with her brow in shadow. Death
hovered above her. Listening to the breath
catch in her throat I heard the boy's sweet song.

The child was five, his laughter and his games
there by the window filled the room with joy.
Worn out, the mother near her charming boy
who sang all day long coughed away the night.

She went to sleep beneath a slab of stone.
The boy opened his mouth again and sang.
Grief is a fruit God won't allow to hang
from any branch too slight to bear the weight.

Paris, January 1835

Unity

Over the skyline of burnished hills
the sun flowering on boundless splendour
lingered above earth before setting;
a humble daisy by the field's edge
on a grey wall crumbling where the oats
grew wild spread, white, its spotless halo
and the little flower staring over
the old wall at the vast star shedding
ageless light through the eternal blue
said to the sun 'I have got rays too.'

Granville, July 1836

The First of May

All conjugates the verb 'to love'. Look – roses!
I'm in no mood to speak of other things.
The first of May! Love, sad, gay, jealous, ardent,
brings sighs from wood and nest, from flowers and wolves.
The tree I carved a motto on last autumn
repeats my words and thinks it's made them up.
The old caves deep in thought, mocked by each jay,
half-close their eyes, allow their mouths a smirk.
The air is scented, gentle, seeming filled
with promises the meadow says to spring
or vows the grass in love offers the clouds.
At every move the day makes in the sky,
the countryside, more lovestruck every hour,
lavishes fragrance, tells the milder breeze
to pass its kisses on to June while blossoms
stain everywhere you look with colour,
with blue, with carmine, purple, saffron – their breath
takes flight in murmurings of love
on cliffs, ponds, turf and new-ploughed fields: the land
has given scents away but kept the flowers
as though its letters, sent with sighs to May,
left telltale traces on the blotter's page –
and spring now laughing in the wayward boughs
enjoys each message of outspoken love.
The birds, their voices muffled by the leaves,
sing rondeaux to the elves. And everything
is telling secrets to the shade and is
in love, admitting it in whispers.
                                        You'd say
that to the north – the vivid south –
where sunset flares or daybreak whitens –
the hedge in flower, the ivy, and the source
that drips in echoes down the rock,
the hills, the fields, the lakes, the swaying oaks
repeat four lines invented by four winds.

Queen Omphalé's Spinning-Wheel

It stands in the atrium, of fine ivory.
The tensely balanced wheel is white,
the distaff black.
It stands on a rich carpet in the atrium.
Lapis lazuli encrusts
the distaff of black ebony.

A sculptor from Aegina carved the plinth.
Europa's lament goes
unheeded by the god. The white bull
carries her away. She cries
devoid of hope then lowering her gaze
with horror sees her pink feet kissed
by the monstrous sea.

There are needles and thread and boxes
with lids half-closed.
Wool from Miletos dyed purple and gold
spills from one basket though the wheel
hangs still.

Meanwhile,
in the depths of the palace,
ghosts of a score of half-seen monsters
enormous, repellent, frightening,
blood-stained,
crowd together circling
the quiet spinning-wheel –
the lion from Nemea, the Lernæan hydra,
Cacus the dark brigand of the dark cave,
the triple-bodied Geryon
and the water-things
that hiss at evening through the reeds.

The mark of the club has stamped each brow
and they prowl not daring to draw
nearer the wheel where one
supple thread is wound
but linger far off gazing
humiliated from the gloom.

Letter

From here you can see –
                              ochre; chalkwhite;
broad fields striped by the plough;
hedges masking
thatched roofs that hug the ground;
some haystacks standing on grass;
smoke from old chimneys
darkening the tan landscape;
an undramatic Norman stream
tidal with salt from the near sea –
on the right, towards the north,
geometries of land as weird
as if a shovel hacked them out.
That's the foreground – pricked
by an old chapel and a few
tortuous elms weary
with reproaching the continual wind.
A large cart rusts
by the corner of the house.
Before me there's one vast
horizon and the blue sea
filling all the notches in the coast.
Chickens cackle and cocks
flaunt their gold tails
under my window. Songs in dialect
are lobbed from the hayloft.
An old man, a rope-maker,
lives next door – I hear
the noise of his wheel and watch
as he backs
out of his shed, the end of the hemp
coiled round his waist.

I love the waves here and the wind
distracted over them. I walk
all day long in the fields. I lodge
with the village schoolmaster

and envious children, book in hand,
watch me play truant.
The sky's one laughter, the air
is pure filled all day with the sweet
noises of the class
spelling their words aloud.
Water runs by, a greenfinch
passes, I give thanks to God –
this is the way I'm living,
peacefully,
taking the hour as it comes,
letting my days trickle away drop
by drop and thinking of you, my love,
my fair one.
I listen to the children chatter
and occasionally, out at sea,
passing superb above these quiet
gables, I'll see the sails
of a great ship bound
for the long ocean
tracked by the winds.
Last week she'll have lain
sleeping against the quayside
far from the jealous waves –
though nothing could restrain her, not
parental tears,
wives in their terror,
dark glide of reefs beneath the water,
nor all the warnings given by the birds.

'Come – an unseen flute . . .'

Come – an unseen flute
sighs in the orchard.
    The quietest song
the song that shepherds sing.

The wind beneath the ilex
disturbs the pool's dark glass.
    The happiest song
the song that thrushes sing.

You're anxious still. But love
is ours, is always ours.
    The sweetest song
the song that lovers sing.

Words Spoken in the Shadows

She'd say, 'The hours go very sweetly by.
    'I'm wrong in wanting more, I know.
'You're there. My gaze has never left your eye
'Where I can watch the thoughts that come and go.

'To see you is my joy – though never whole.
    'It's still delightful, to be sure.
'My ear's attentive, for I know my rôle –
'To stop the bores from bursting through the door.

'I sit in my own corner out of sight.
    'You are my lion. I'm your dove.
'I hear the papers rustle as you write
'And stoop to pick your pen up too, my love.

'I have you, to be sure. I see you there.
    'Thought is a drug and those who spend
'Their time in dreams forget. I know. But spare
'One thought for me those evenings when you bend

'Over your books and never speak to me.
    'Shadows cast on my heart remain,
'My love. For me to see you properly
'You must look at me too now and again.'

One Evening When I Was Looking at the Sky

Smiling she said, 'My dearest, why
study the flying day,
the shadows drooping or the gold star
lifting in the east? Up there
is no place for a man's eyes, leave
the sky now, look here at your love.

'You measurelessly read
the vast sky broadening with shade.
What can you learn that matches my smile?
What can you learn that would outdo
our kisses? Turn to me. Take the veil
from a heart where all stars shine for you.

'In love we've suns enough and all
within us glows. Devotion lighting
its way round every obstacle
is worth Venus glittering above the hill.
The immense blue firmament is nothing
compared with the spaces in my soul.

'There's beauty when a star emerges
in the sky. The world is full of wonders.
Sweet is the dawn and sweet are the roses.
But nothing's sweeter than the delight
of love. Two souls exchanging light
with one another make the best of fires.

'Love is worth more, in some cool grove,
than all the suns we name and do not know.
God realized man's need and so
he placed the sky far off, woman close by.
To those who scan the dark above
He says, 'Live. Love. The rest's my mystery.'

'Let's love. That's all. It is God's will.
Leave the cold rays of light that shine

along the sky. In these eyes of mine
there is more beauty and more gold.
To love is to see, know, dream and feel
the spirit nobler and the heart more mild.

'My love, with me you'll understand
this strange music all about us.
Nature transformed in harmony
now sings our love. Come, take my hand
and stroll with me over the grass.
I've become so jealous of the sky.'

My love spoke thus, her sweet voice low,
white hand placed on her brow
like an angel in a dream,
grave, ever-lovely, calm;
content to be with me like this,
her sweet voice low, my love spoke thus.

Our hearts were beating in rapture.
The evening flowers opened. What have the woods,
I wonder, done with our words,
the rocks with our sighs?
Man's fate is sad when such days
pass that none can recapture.

Memory – treasure heaped in shade,
dark skyline of thoughts long dead,
fond gleam from objects now eclipsed,
glow of former days that have vanished –
her temple lets the mind's eye behold
the past only from the threshold.

When fine days yield to bitter ones
you must relinquish every thought
of joy. Drain the last of hope
then into the ocean drop the cup.
Forgetfulness – the wave where all drowns,
the dark sea where you cast delight.

Written Beneath a Crucifix

All those in tears, approach this God in tears.
All those in pain, approach because He heals.
All those in fear, approach because He smiles.
All those who pass, approach for He endures.

March 1842

On the Plinth of an Ancient Bas-Relief

to Mademoiselle Louise B.

Music is present in all things. There is a hymn
that issues from the world.
                              Slap of the waves
against the galley's side, the noise of towns, pity shown
by one sister to another, beauty of first lovers
in their passion, the gentleness of an old couple
together worn by life in its movement past them,
fanfares of summer when fields are dotted with flowers,
words exchanged at evening on brotherly doorsteps,
the darkness trembling among the foliage of ageless oaks –
these are the essence of music and harmony –
these are the sighs providing the ultimate song.

Each new day, the lives we lead, the four seasons,
dreams deep in our hearts, the fold of the skyline,
tears of daybreak and vast fires of evening in the sky –
float in a counterpoint of uncertain melodies.
One voice speaks to us from the meadow, a different voice
sings something else for man far in the forest.
At times there is bleating in the flock or a bell tolls.
When at nightfall the hills are captured by shadow
a dazzling measure of music intertwines dancing
through all the sky to the height of the starry zenith,
through the irregular call of birds and cry of cicadas.
Sweet sounds have always paired off with our hearts.
Nature tells us to sing and this is the reason why
the ancient sculptor carved here on this stone
a shepherd whose eyes are lowered, rapt, as he plays his flute.

June 1833

'The bright air outside . . .'

The bright air outside does not deflect me.
The countryside may well laugh like a young
    woman. In the holly
a nest flutters. The world is open-mouthed
with happiness, on every side songs blaze
    in joy. Spring, stretched at ease
on moss in the shadow of green clearings,
    watches lovers fondly.

Over fields of lucerne and in gardens
where scarlet beans are flowering, unsteady
    butterflies drift like dreams.
Green wheat is sprouting from the brown furrows.
Golden bees speed to blue clumps of blossom,
    to the sweet-smelling thyme,
to the bindweed that offers its white cups
    so they can drink its scent.

Each cloud displays its purple, its copper.
Trees, swollen with May, look drunk – their branches
    making the regular
gestures of some charming game are tossing
the birds to each other like shuttlecocks.
    The bumble-bee in stripes
of black and yellow murmurs suggestions
    to the coquettish rose.

But I, indifferent to this fragrance, let
    the wind blow all the splendour where it will –
    let the sweet ghosts of flowers
whisper together, daybreak say, 'You'll live.'
I look into myself, alone, forget
    what time it is and then,
filled with the knowledge of the dark in things,
    I think of the free dead.

A little while will pass, the proud sea ebb
and flow again a few more times before
    I also have my grave,
a blank space among the fresh grass, shaded
by some tree twisted about with ivy.
    The passer-by will read
these words: This slab of stone hides from your eyes
the ruin of a gaol.

Ingouville, May 1843

'A little girl . . .'

A little girl sees her granny spinning.
She wants a hank of flax for her doll
and bides her time.
There! Granny's nodding off,
so she steals up, pulls
a strand as the bobbin spins,
and triumphant skips away
with some wool dyed saffron gold –
about as much as a bird would take
building its nest.

Cauterets, 25 August 1843

'Spider, nettle, loathed . . .'

Spider, nettle, loathed –
hence loved by me.
Punished, their pitiful
needs ungranted, they're
miserable, accursed,
mean things of darkness, sad
captives of their own nature,
snared, fatally
snared in the coil
of their actions.
           The nettle's
hated like a snake, the spider
avoided like a leper.
Shadows of the abyss
hang over them. The shunned.
The victims of the night.

As you pass by, feel
sorrow for their secret,
their poverty and spare
this plant, this spider.
Pity their ugliness. Pity
the fact this nettle
has to sting. Take
pity on evil.

There's nothing
without its sadness.
All that lives
craves affection.
           Consider
these two, untamed, repellent –
supposing you simply
passed by forgetting
to squash them under your feet,

supposing you simply
looked at them showing
less scorn – then
both of them,
the ugly creature and the weed,
softly,
far from the light of day,
would marvel murmuring
at this proof of your love.

July 1842

'She formed the habit . . .'

She formed the habit in her earliest years
of coming to my room each morning so
I'd wait for her as you might hope for light.
She'd enter, say hello, take up my pen,
open my books, sit on my bed, disturb
my papers, laugh – then leave abruptly as
a bird that passes. Easier then in mind
I'd take up what she'd interrupted till
among my manuscripts I'd come across
some funny arabesque she'd scribbled or
a few blank pages which she'd crumpled up –
and somehow, though I don't know why, on these
would always come my most successful lines.
She loved our God, loved flowers, stars, green fields –
pure spirit long before she was a woman!
Her eyes mirrored the brightness of her soul.
She'd tend to ask me what I thought of things –
so many radiant winter evenings spent
discussing history or points of language,
four children grouped around my knees, their mother
close by, some friends too chatting near the fire.
I called that life being content with little.
And now she's dead. God help me. How could I
be happy when I knew that she was sad?
I was despondent at the gayest ball
if earlier I'd seen shadows in her eyes.

November 1846, All Souls' Day

'On our hills of the past . . .'

On our hills of the past
when we all lived together
in that house by the wood
where the streams run, where
the bushes tremble –
she was ten, I was thirty
and for her the whole world.

How fragrant the grass now
under the huge green trees.

Because of her my life
was thriving, work
went easily, my skies were blue.
She thanked me, her father.
I gave thanks for her to God.
I heard her joyous words
through my uncounted dreams
and in the gloom of thought my brow
took light from her eyes.

She looked like a princess
when I took her by the hand.
She walked along those paths
searching for flowers, seeking out
the poor. She gave as others
steal, first making sure
no one was looking.

Do you remember the dress
she used to wear, how
pretty it was?
                    At dusk,
near my candle,
she'd prattle softly on while moths
struck the reddened pane.

Angels admired themselves in her.
The simplest greeting on her lips
had charm. In her pupils heaven
had placed the look that never lies.

When she appeared in my life
I was young still –
she was the child of my sunrise,
my morning star.

In summer when the moon
shone bright, serene, we'd run
through the fields and woods,
then back along the valley where,
turning the corner by the old wall,
we'd see a single light
starring the dark house.
We'd come back, hearts on fire,
talking of the sky's splendour –
I helped her store her mind
as bees pack hives with honey.

She was so good, so pure, her thoughts
clear as her glance, she was
gay whenever she arrived . . .
All this has passed
like shadows, like the wind.

Villequier, 4 September 1844
[first anniversary of Léopoldine's death]

Veni, Vidi, Vixi

I have lived long enough, since in my grief
　　nobody's arm will aid me as I walk,
since I cannot join in when children laugh,
　　since I derive no pleasure now from flowers,

Since in the spring when life starts to delight
　　with God, I stand aside and feel no joy,
since I have reached the time when men flee light
　　and know the secret sadness of all things,

Since every hope is vanquished in my breast,
　　since in this month when roses scent the air
I crave the shade where you, my daughter, rest,
　　since my heart's dead I have lived long enough.

I've not refused my earthly business –
　　my furrow? There. And here my sheaf of corn.
I have lived smiling and learned gentleness,
　　stood upright, though inclined to mystery.

I've done all that I could. I've served, kept watch,
　　though often seen the world deride my pains,
amazed to find so many showing such
　　hatred for me who suffered labouring.

In this terrestrial gaol where no wing soars –
　　bleeding, without complaint, down on my hands,
fatigued, the butt of every prisoner's jeers –
　　I've borne my link of the eternal chain.

And now my eyelids stay half-closed. I turn
　　my head no longer when my name is called.
I'm filled with sloth and tedium like a man
　　who rises before dawn and has not slept.

In sombre lethargy I hear the spite
   on tongues of slanderers and don't reply.
Oh Lord, unfasten now the gates of night
   that I may take my leave and disappear.

April 1848

'At dawn, tomorrow . . .'

At dawn, tomorrow, when the landscape's whitening,
I shall set off. You are expecting me.
I'll take the forest road, the upland road.
I can't go on living so far from you.

I'll walk, eyes focused on my thoughts,
the world around unseen, its sounds unheard,
alone, unrecognized, back bent, hands folded,
saddened; for me day will be as the dark.

I shall not watch the gold as evening falls
nor distant sails downstream towards Harfleur
and on arrival I'll place on your grave
a wreath of holly twined with heather-flowers.

3 September 1847

Words Spoken on the Dunes

The time left to me sputters like a spent torch,
    the tasks I had to do are over,
I have been driven by the years, by mourning,
    up to the very brink of the grave.

I had my soaring dreams – now across the sky
    so many hours that struck in the past
with beauty are scudding towards the darkness
    like clouds of dust before the whirlwind.

I have learnt to say, 'One day we know triumph –
    and on the next all fades to falsehood.'
I am weighed with sadness like a dreamer bent
    double walking here beside these waves.

Above the hill, the valley and the endless
    stirring of the sea I watch the north
wind with a vulture's beak tearing the fleece off
    the flock of clouds trying to escape.

I hear the breeze move through the air and the tide
    shift against the rocks and the voices
of farmers as they bind the ripe sheaves of corn
    and all these sounds are blended to one.

Sometimes I lie unmoving among the sparse
    tufts of grass on the sand-dunes until
the moment arrives for moonrise and her blurred
    rings gaze out at me like hollow eyes.

She climbs, throws a long inactive ray of light
    on space, nature's mystery, the sea,
and we stare unblinking at each other, I
    the sufferer, she the bright silent moon.

Where have my vanished days all gone? Is there one
    man left who can tell me who I am?
And do my dazzled eyes retain anything
    of the radiance I had in my youth?

All's disappeared. I am alone, I am tired.
    I call and no one replies. I hear
the breeze, the sea, and I myself am no more
    than a breath of wind or a swift wave.

Shall I never see again what I once loved?
    The night is falling now in my heart.
Mist is hiding the higher ground and the earth
    is like a grave and I am its ghost.

Have I drained each cup – of life, of love, of joy,
    of hope? What answer may I implore
as I tip each one on to its side to try
    to catch the last drop remaining there.

Memory stays but memories bring remorse.
    All we think of takes us back to tears.
Death is the black bolt that shuts the door on man.
    I feel how cold it is to the touch.

Deep in thought I listen to the bitter wind
    and the waves that cut me from my home –
summer is alive with laughter, by the shore
    the sea-holly is showing blue flowers.

    5 August 1854
    [*second anniversary of Hugo's arrival on Jersey*]

Shepherds and Their Flocks

to Madame Louise C.

Each day I go down a charming valley,
    remote, serene, lonely
beneath the sky, filled with brambles in flower,
    a place of sad smiles where
you can forget that other things exist.
    The sound of men working
in the fields is the only reminder
    life's going on elsewhere.
The shadows there make love and nature's own
    idyll creates laughter
as bullfinches quarrel with linnets or
    the blackcap cocks his head
ready for a fight. Sometimes the hawthorn
    shows its blossom, sometimes
the yellow broom; outcrops of black granite
    give way to the bright moss:
God places contrasting effects of light
    and shade for like Homer
He repeats Himself – though with flowers and hills,
    with water and the woods.
One small pool has wrinkles on its surface
    and to the passing ant
they're waves. The sea roaring far off can't see
    this irony displayed
in the grass. There is a sweet girl sometimes
    sitting on the gnarled rock.
She's fifteen, blue-eyed, barefoot. Her job is
    looking after the goats.
Her home is along a black narrow path,
    an ancient tumbledown
cottage where in the evening the lamplight
    makes stars among the thatch.
Her sisters stay behind and spin. She dries
    her feet wet from the pool
on rushes. Her goats, her ewes, her rams graze
    quietly. When my dark form

approaches, the poor angel is afraid
and smiles at me as I
greet her, the example of innocence.
Lambs bound in the meadow
sanctified with the scent of flowers and when
the sun turns to scarlet
they leave on the bushes tufts of white wool
that float as the wind comes
like flakes of foam. I move on and the child,
her flock, lose their outlines
in mist. Twilight stretches over the long
grey furrows its ghost wings,
its bat wings, and still I hear behind me
the sweet girl's song far off
across the tilled fields. There in front of me
the headland capped with clouds
seems to be guarding the expanse of foam,
the reef and the seaweed,
the endless swaying of the waves, and like
a giant lost in thought
or a shepherd leaning on his elbow
it dreams among the noise
of wind and sea at the edge of the world
and, as the clouds rise blessed
along the sky, sees the triumphant moon
lift from the horizon
as shadows tremble and harsh gusts of air
disperse the tufts of spray
left by the dark beasts that make up the sea.

Jersey, Grouville, April 1855

What Death Is

Do not say 'dead'; say 'born'. Believe. We all
can see what I see, what you see. We're all
as bad as I am, as you are. We rush
to dizzy pleasures of the world, forget
that we descend through danger to the end,
the grave, the dark republic of our sins,
although the small man's equal to the rich,
for all are sons of the same father, we
are all the same tears wept by the same eye.
We live and wear our days out filled with pride.
We walk and run and dream, feel pain and fall
and rise. What is this dawn? It is the tomb.

Where am I then? In death. An unknown wind
hurls you to heaven's threshold where you tremble,
naked, impure, bound with a thousand chains –
with wrongs committed, shameful sins, the dark.
And then you hear across the infinite
a voice that singing says you're blessed. We can
not see the hand that sheds on our sick soul
its love, we cannot know the voice that sings.
We come as men – in grief – like snow. We melt
and live and filled with the blue shine of bliss
we quiver during that bizarre defeat
when monsters turn to angels in the light.

by the dolmen de la tour Blanche, All Souls' Day, 1854

Nomen, Numen, Lumen

When he had finished, when the scattered suns
climbed dazzled out of chaos to arrange
themselves throughout the spreading deeps of space,
feeling it right to give the world his name
the calm tremendous being rose and stood
against the dark to cry aloud JEHOVAH
and in the vastness seven letters fell
to form reflected in our eyes each night
shimmering down upon our upturned brows
the seven giant stars that show the north.

Midnight, by the le Faldouet dolmen, 1 March 1855

The Consecration of Woman

I

A dawn was breaking, an abyss
that dazzled, fathomless, sublime –
one blaze of peace.
It was the world's first age. Across the sky,
serenely out of reach, a brightness showed
all that is ever visible of God.
All grew in light – shadows, darkened mist –
beneath a toppling avalanche of gold.
The day set fire to all the far
reaches of life that lay along the ravished
centre of the world.
The distance flashed with miracles
as in a dream, horizons shone
spinning their shadows and their tufted rocks
and their fantastic trees since vanished from the world.
Eden, bare, chaste, was softly
coming awake. Birds warbled songs like hymns
so full of grace and tenderness, so fresh,
the angels idly leaned across to hear.
The tiger's roar was gentler then
and melody was limitless.
Groves where the lambs grazed
side by side with wolves,
seas where serpents glided in peace
past the sleeping halcyon, plains
where bears and the fallow-deer
allowed their breath to mingle
poised hesitating
between the call from the cave's mouth
and the song rising from the nest.
Prayer seemed the same as light.
The morning, murmuring some sacred phrase,
smiled as dawn threw a halo
round nature still immaculate that still
hummed with the sound of the eternal word –
round a world that stayed

celestial, seraphic, innocent.
The face of happiness remained intact.
No mouth held poison and no thing
lacked primal majesty.
All that the infinite could hurl of light
burst random through the air –
the wind, grasping that sheaf of glory,
tossed it in play among the dissipating
whirl of clouds.
Hell tried a few stammered snorts of scorn
that were absorbed in one great shout of joy
from streams and hills and woods and earth and sky.
The breezes and the sunshine sowed delight.
The forests thrilled like lyres. A sense
of brotherhood and praise
spread from the blackness to the light,
from base to summit. Stars had no arrogance
and worms no envy. Through the vast
spectrum of existence there ran love.
A harmony equalling the light that poured
divinity upon the youthful earth
issued from the mysterious
heart of the world. The grass was stirred,
the cloud, the wave,
even the dreaming rock that holds its peace.
The trees transfixed by light rustled with song.
Each flower received a pearl of dew
and offered fragrance to the air.
Creation was all
splendour, all unity. Paradise shone
beneath dark branches where life
murmured in rapture. The light
was made of truth.
All things had grace for they had purity.
And all was celebration,
marriage of fire and mercy, each
of these dawns of vastness
heralded one vast day.

How to describe that first gold ray
which throwing light on everything
knew nothing yet:
morning of mornings, love, the unbridled joy
of starting time, of starting hour and month and year,
the opening of the world, instant of wonder
as night dissolved in the enormous sky
and there was neither fear nor weeping
and no pain. Light was a gulf now
huge as chaos. The calm grandeur of God
was displayed as sureness for the soul
and glory for the eye. From height
to height, in air, on earth through all
the countless twists and turns deep
in the strata of existence, light
burst in adoration.
The world was outline. All had paused
to think out the next step. First creatures blending
the half-brute with the half-angel
rose stormy, gigantic, blurred,
and underneath these jumbled groups the earth
kept seething, an untiring womb.
Hallowed creation, creator in its turn,
sketched fabulous designs, brought swarms
of legendary monsters from the woods
and seas and clouds, suggesting different
shapes to God which time,
reflecting on this harvest, later changed.
Within the greening of enormous leaves
all future trees were starting to emerge –
pine, maple, ilex. A sort of excess life
was swelling the earth's great udder
filled with secret milk. Things seemed
to hatch or blossom almost out of scale
as if nature – still too close to chaos –
had taken from it for her tests on land and sea
a splendid shapelessness.

The earthly paradise, running with rare sap,
glows dream-like in the long-lost depths of time.
Its ecstasies today would terrify
our feebler eyes that lack ideals or faith.
What does this matter to the universal soul
that squanders suns like sparks
and so an angel winged with sky can walk there
builds Eden high until it touches heaven!

Days past imagining –
the good, the fine, the true, the just
flowed in the torrent, rustled in each bush.
The north wind robed in wisdom praised the Lord.
Each tree knew kindness and each flower was virtue.
Lilies, not merely white, showed candour.
Nothing was blemished, nothing wrinkled.
Pure days – no claw, no fang drew blood.
Each happy animal was innocence on the prowl.
The mystery of evil had not yet involved
the lofty eagle nor the snake nor panther;
light reached the depths of every sacred creature's mind;
no darkness marred the corner of a soul.
Each hill was young, each wave was virginal.
The globe emerging each day from the tide
was beautiful and proud and filled with love.
Nothing was little although everything
was childlike.
Earth among her hymns of purity
was dazed with the thrill of sap and growing things.
A fertile instinct set a dream amid
the instinct for survival. Love,
scattered everywhere, on water, in the wind,
drifted like a fragrance.
Nature was laughter – innocent, immense.
Space whimpered like a new-born baby.
Dawn was the glance of an astonished sun.

Now that day was the loveliest
a radiant sunrise ever shed
upon the universe.
The same divine shimmer ran
through the seaweed and the wave,
the being and its element.
The upper air shone with a greater purity.
The mountain-tops abounded in a wealth
of sweeter breezes, the foliage
stirred with added grace
and rays of light caressed one cool
green valley where,
in overflow of ecstasy,
in worship of the sky inflamed with light,
content to be, happy to love,
entranced with what they saw,
there in the shade beside a lake so calm
it formed a dizzying mirror for the sky –
the first man sat by the first woman
their feet touching the clear water.

The husband was praying, his wife at his side.

IV

Eve offered the blue day her naked sanctity.
Eve, blonde, admired the blushes of her sister, dawn.

A woman's flesh is the ideal clay
and born of miracle. Spirit
imbues matter which God has kneaded
for the soul shines through its earthly covering
and on her body you can see
where the fingers of the divine
sculptor have left their mark.
This dust, given such majesty,
summons the kiss, the heart,
and is so sacred that, vanquished by love,

impelled towards her bed of mystery,
you wonder whether sensuality
is not the same as thought –
so sacred that,
when all your senses are on fire,
you can't clasp beauty in your arms
without the notion you're embracing God.

Eve let her eyes stray over Eden.

Beneath the high green palm-trees
carnations seemed to dream around Eve's head.
The dark blue lotus pondered, the forget-me-not
thought back and roses inclined their blooms
to kiss her feet.
The lily tinged with sunrise breathed out fragrance.
It was as if Eve had been one of them,
as if of all these flowers, each with its soul,
the loveliest had blossomed into woman.

V

Yet up till now Adam was the elect.
He'd been the first to read the sacred sky.
The man, tranquil and strong, had been the one
whom light and shadow, dawn, the unnumbered stars,
the creatures of the wood, the flowers of the ravine
followed or worshipped as an elder brother,
touched with divinity, whose forehead held
a higher gleam than theirs –
and when they both walked hand in hand
across the joy of Eden's radiance,
nature – from rock and bough and stream and grass-blade –
watched lovingly the beauty of the pair
(Eve looking, Adam meditating)
but felt respect more deeply for the man.
That day, however, countless eyes –
those of the infinite concealed – were fixed
upon the woman, not the man –
as though on that gentle religious day,

blessed among all days, among all dawns,
the nests concealed under echoing branches,
the clouds and rivulets and shimmering swarms,
the animals and stones, all things that then
were holy though today they lie
hidden beneath the shadows of our words,
believed the woman nobler than the man.

VI

And why this choice? Why should
the firmament deflect
vast tenderness? Why should
the universe be bending now
over one head? the dawn
be celebrating woman?
Why all this song? Why are the waves
glittering in increase of joy?
Why rapture everywhere and why
this haste to blossom?
Why are the caverns eager to admit
the growing light? Why is there more
fragrance about the earth,
more flaming in the sky?

The beautiful pair stayed silent,
reflective in their innocence.

VII

Meanwhile the unutterable
gentleness of the sun, the green valley,
the lake, each leaf of moss
trembled more deeply, more intensely,
moment by moment gathering round Eve as day
did homage to her from the radiance of the sky.
The gaze that issued from all things, all beings –
from sacred waves, the holy woods,
the priestly trees –
became more fixed, more pensive,

looking with veneration at this woman
whose forehead held such charm.
A long ray of love
reached her from the distance of the air,
from the shadow, from the blueness of the sky,
from depth and height, from flowers,
from birds in song, from quiet stones.

And, pale, Eve felt a stirring in her womb.

5–17 October 1858

Conscience

With all his children dressed in coats of skins,
Dishevelled, while the thunder crashed above,
Cain hastened from the presence of the Lord.
At nightfall, Cain, branded with darkness, came
Down the long mountainside on to a plain.
His wife and sons, exhausted, said to him,
'Let us lie down upon the ground and sleep.'
Cain did not sleep, brooding among the rocks.
He raised his head and in the livid sky
He saw an eye, wide open in the dark,
Unblinking, fixed on him among the shadows.
'I'm still too near then,' he said shivering.
He woke his wife and children from their rest,
Moved on to set more darkened space behind him.
He went for thirty days and thirty nights,
In silence, pale, and trembling at each sound,
Furtive, without a glance behind. No pause.
No rest. No sleep. At last he reached the shore
Of that land which has since been called Assur.
'We'll halt,' he said. 'This sanctuary is sure.
'Stop now. We've found the limit of the world.'
And as he sat he saw in the bleak sky
The eye in the same place on the horizon.
And then he shuddered, gripped by sunless fear.
'Hide me,' he screamed. Their fingers on their lips
His sons and grandsons watched the old man shake.
Cain said to Jabal, father of those who dwell
In tents of camel-hair on the vast desert,
'Stretch out the cloth on this side like a screen.
When they'd unrolled it flapping in the wind
And fixed it taut with weights of lead, Zillah,
Fair child, the daughter of his sons, as sweet
As sunrise, said, 'Can you see anything?'
And Cain replied, 'I can still see the eye.'
Jubal, father of those who blow on trumpets
And striking drums make music in the towns,
Cried out, 'I can construct a barrier.'

He made a wall of bronze in front of Cain.
Cain said, 'The eye is looking at me still.'
So Enoch said, 'We'll set a ring of towers
'So terrible that no one dare approach.
'Let's build a town with a high citadel.
'We'll build a town and then we'll close it off.'
Then Tubal-cain, the father of all blacksmiths,
Constructed a vast superhuman city.
And while he worked his brothers drove away
The sons of Enos and the sons of Seth.
If anyone came near they put his eyes out.
At night they shot their arrows at the stars.
Granite replaced the cloth walls of the tent.
Each block was clamped in place with knots of iron.
The town was like a place conceived in hell.
Its towers cast night upon the countryside.
The walls were thick as mountains. On the gate
These words were carved: *God is forbidden here.*
When they had finished walling round the town,
They put Cain in the centre in a tower
Of stone. Face drawn and pale, he entered. 'Father,'
Asked Zillah trembling, 'Has it gone away?'
And Cain then answered, 'No. The eye's still there.'
He said, 'I want to live below the ground
'Like men alone, deep in their sepulchres.
'Nothing will see me. I'll see nothing there.'
They dug a pit and Cain said, 'It is good.'
Then by himself he went down to the dark.
And when he took his seat among the shadows,
And when they'd fixed the heavy slab in place,
The eye was in the tomb and looked at Cain.

Boaz Asleep

Boaz was overcome with weariness.
All day he'd laboured on the threshing-floor,
then made his bed in his accustomed place.
He slept now by the bushels full of corn.

He had great fields of barley and of wheat.
And he was just, although a wealthy man.
The water from his mills ran clean and free,
his forges burned without a flame from hell.

His beard was silver like an April stream.
A tight fist never bound his harvest-sheaves –
he'd say each time he saw a woman gleaning,
'Drop ears of corn on purpose for the poor.'

He walked with candour, far from subtle paths,
robed in white linen and in probity.
His grain-sacks ever open for the needy
flowed plentifully as the public fountains.

A worthy master and a loyal kinsman
he was, though generous, not a squanderer.
Women admired him more than younger men –
young men have beauty but the old have grandeur.

Old men, returning to the source of life,
leave changing days and enter timelessness.
There may be fire in eyes of younger men
but in the eyes of old men there is light.

*

So Boaz slept that night among his own.
And near the stacks of hay like alien mounds
the groups of harvesters lay in the shadows.
And this was in the very ancient times

when judges led the tribes of Israel.
Men lived in tents and wandered anxiously
seeing the prints left by a giant foot –
the earth was wet and soft still from the flood.

*

As Jacob slept and Holofernes slept
Boaz lay underneath the summer leaves.
Above his head the gates of heaven opened
        and a dream descended.

The dream was such that Boaz saw an oak
that sprouted from his belly to the sky.
A race of men climbed up it in a chain –
there was a king that sang, a god who died.

And Boaz murmured questions in his heart:
'How can these wonders issue out of me?
'The number of my years has passed four score.
'I have no wife now and I have no son.

'For she who shared my bed has long ago
'abandoned, Lord, my household for your own.
'And we are still a part of one another –
'she lives in me and I am dead with her.

'A race sprung from my loins! How could that be?
'I can't believe that I'll have children now.
'When you are young you have triumphant dreams –
'day comes from night as from a victory –

'but, old, you shiver like a birch in winter.
'I'm widowed and alone, dusk falls on me
'and I lean now above the open grave
'as thirsty oxen bend towards the pool.'

        Boaz spoke thus in dream
and turned to God, his eyes immersed in sleep.
No cedar sees a rose bloom at its base.
He did not see a woman at his feet.

*

While he was sleeping, Ruth, a Moabite,
had come to lie bare-breasted at his feet,
half-hoping for some unknown ray of light
when sudden dawn illumined all the world.

Boaz had no idea that she was there
and Ruth had no idea what God desired.
A cool scent rose from tufts of asphodel.
The night air stirred soft over Galgala.

All shadows floated, nuptial, stately, grave.
And surely angels flew in secrecy
for through the night from time to time you'd see
a shift of azure looking like a wing.

The quiet breath of Boaz as he slept
merged with the stream that rippled over moss.
It was the month when nature is most sweet,
when all the hills have lilies on their crests.

Ruth dreamed while Boaz slept. The grass was dark.
The bells shook gently on the distant flocks.
A vast well-being fell from heaven like dew.
It was the hour when lions go and drink.

All was at peace in Ur and Jerimoth.
Stars glimmered in the black depths of the sky.
The crescent moon shone in the west among
the constellations scattered there like flowers

and Ruth was wondering through half-opened eyes
what harvester of the eternal summer
when going home had carelessly thrown down
that golden sickle on the field of stars.

1 May 1859

Christ's First Encounter with the Tomb

In those days Jesus was in Judæa.
He had loosed the woman from the bonds
of her infirmity, opened
the ears of the deaf, and lepers
had left his presence cleansed.

The priests kept watch, speaking
among themselves in low voices.

As he was returning to Jerusalem,
the holy city,
a man of Bethany named Lazarus
fell sick and died. He had
two sisters, Mary and Martha. One day,
Mary, to anoint the feet
of their visitor, the Lord of Love,
had fetched a precious ointment.
Now Jesus loved Martha,
and her sister, and Lazarus.
And someone came to him saying,
Lazarus is dead.
        Next day,
as a great crowd came to meet him,
he expounded the law to them, the scriptures,
and the symbols of belief, speaking,
like Elijah and like Job, in parables.
He said, Who follows me
walks on the way of angels.
If a man travel all day in the sun
on a dry road with no well and no shelter
when evening comes, if he has no faith,
he cries and is afraid, he is weary
and falls panting to the ground.
If he believes in me he prays and then
continues, thrice-strong, on his journey.
He then broke off and said to his disciples,

Lazarus, our friend, is sleeping. I
shall awake him. The disciples said,
Wherever you go, Master, we
will follow.
Now Bethany lies many leagues
from Jerusalem where the Ark is housed
and the journey takes three days.
Jesus set off. While he walked
his white clothes shone from time to time
with light.
When he arrived, Martha ran up
and falling at his feet cried, Master,
if you had been here, my brother
would not have died. Then added in tears,
But he has given up the ghost. You've come
too late. And Jesus said, Woman,
you do not understand. The harvester alone
is master of the harvest.

Mary still sat in the house.

And Martha called to her, saying,
The Master needs you. So she came
and Jesus said, Why are you in tears?
And Mary knelt and said, I know,
Master, you alone are strong.
If you were here, my brother
had not died.
Jesus said, I am the light and the life.
Happy the man who follows where I walk.
He that believes in me shall live
though he were dead and in his grave.
And Thomas, called the Twin, was present.

The Lord then, standing with John and Peter,
addressed the crowd of Jews, saying,
Where have you laid him?
They pointed to a field near a wood
where a stream ran among stones.

There was a tomb there.
                    And Jesus wept.

The crowd said, See how he loved him.
People say he casts out devils.
If he were God as we are told
would he have allowed his friend to die?

Martha led Jesus to the tomb.
A stone sealed the door. And Martha said,
I believe in you as John and Peter do,
but my brother has been beneath that stone
four days.
                    And Jesus said,
Be silent now. In this place, if you believe,
you will see the glory of God.
And he said, Take away the stone.
And they saw the inside of the tomb.
And Jesus, raising his eyes to heaven,
entered the darkness where the corpse
lay in its shroud like the coins
a miser puts in a sack and buries.
And leaning over it he cried with a loud voice,
Lazarus!
                    The dead man
came from the tomb, his feet still wrapped
in the bindings of his shroud,
and stood against the wall. And Jesus said,
Loose him and let him go.
And all that saw believed.

Now hearing that Christ had raised a man from the dead
and that so many had seen the opening of the tomb,
according to the book the priests were troubled,
and they gathered before the Roman governor, saying,
It is time to put him to death.

Jersey, 23 October 1852

The Rose in the Infanta's Hand

She's very small, there's a duenna at her side,
she holds a rose and looks . . .
at what? She doesn't know – just
what there is in front of her: a pool
beneath murmuring
branches of birch and pine,
a white-winged swan, the whole
flowered sweep of garden.
She's like an angel carved from snow.
A palace ringed in golden light
commands this spreading park where does
drink at the clear ponds
and peacocks flaunt starred tails
under the trailing lines of leaves.
A further whiteness cast by innocence
clusters the light around her,
and her charm trembles, radiant.
The lawn is sewn
with crystal. From the dolphin's carved mouth pours
a cascade of sapphires.
She stands there by the water
studying her flower. She wears
satin trimmed with lace. Gold threads
trace arabesques among the folds.
The full
blossom of the rose seems almost
too heavy for her hand.
She tests its fragrance, kissing it.
The crimson petals half conceal her face:
two royalties – the flower, the child –
so lovely and so similar who's to say
which is the petal, which her cheek?
She has enchantment, fragrance, joy.
Her perfect eyebrows curve in brown,
her eyes are blue. She's called
Maria and her name,
the colour of her gaze,

indicate heaven, though, poor child,
she can't escape a vague sense she is great:
this spring, the play of light and shadow,
the blaze of sunset thrown sidelong,
the purl of unseen water, fields,
undying nature, the entire
magnificence of evening – all
the serene display is hers
and noted with the grave eyes of a queen.
She's never seen a man who didn't bow.
She'll be one day the Duchess of Brabant
and govern Flanders or Sardinia.
She's the Infanta, she is five, she feels disdain.
The children of a king cannot be otherwise –
their brows however fair
have coronets of shadow and their first
few awkward steps mark the beginning of a reign.
She'll breathe her rose until one day
they pluck an empire for her and her glance,
already royal, says, 'That's mine.'
Love steals around her tinged with fear.
She stands defenceless, frail, and yet
if someone – even though to save her – placed
his hand upon her, then
before he'd taken a step or said one word
he'd have the shadow of the scaffold in his eyes.

The sweet child smiles –
all she must do is be alive
and hold a rose
and stand before the sky among her flowers.

The day fades. Nests are filled,
restless, with squabbling.
The sunset's colours lie along each branch.
Stone goddesses begin to blush
seeming to shiver at the approach of night.
Wings that were soaring drop now back to earth.
No noise now, neither light.
The evening's mystery conceals

the sun beneath the distant wave and birds
behind the shelter of a leaf.

And while the child is laughing,
flower in hand,
in the vast palace where
each window apes a bishop's mitre,
someone lurks behind an upper pane,
half hidden –
there is a shadow wrapped in mist
that moves from room to room shedding
fear. Sometimes
this spectre stands daylong
immobile like the form
of darkness in a graveyard,
looking at nothing. He prowls
from one chamber to another,
pale-faced, clothed in black, and puts
his forehead against the glass,
brooding. Wan phantom. Now the fires
of evening throw his longer shadow.
His slow pace echoes like a knell.
It is the image of Death – or else the King.

The King: the man
in whom the nation lives
or trembles leans his shoulder on the wall.
In his dark gaze reflected is no child,
no garden, no stretch of water
shot with the colours of the evening,
no trees for the restive birds – instead,
across those eyes
as secret as the ocean pass
ships, a whole flight of ships swift-
scudding before the wind, sails
billowing, sails
on the foam by starlight, sails
along the distance of the waves
and flickering in the dark.
Far off, an island in the mist

shows a white gleam of cliffs that echo
advancing thunder borne across the sea.

This vision fills the king's cold mind. His eyes
watch nothing round him. This armada
swaying on the tide
will make him master of the earth.
Throughout the gathering dark the king
already conqueror sees the fleet sail on
and a glint of triumph lights his melancholy.

Philip II. Worse than Cain
or Eblis, demon of the Koran.
A royal spectre, son
of the imperial spectre Charles, Philip
was evil in the flesh
and brandishing a sword.
He held his throne as in a nightmare.
No one dared look him in the face.
The weird light of terror shrouded him.
One glimpse of his servant's livery caused
onlookers to shudder. For he
seemed allied to the pit,
to the blue emptiness between the stars.
His will, inhuman,
was like a clamp on fate.
He held America and the Indies, leaned
over Africa, was all-
powerful in Europe – troubled
only about dark England to the north.
His mouth was silence and his soul
enigma. His throne was built
of traps, deceit. He had
the strength of night for his support
and sat astride the dark
like his cold statue on a metal horse.
Omnipotent on earth,
always in black, he seemed
to be in mourning for himself
and like the Sphinx

devoured all questioners and kept
silent, unchanging, for,
as he was everything, he had
no word to say.
No one had seen him smile.
His iron lips
could no more smile than dawnlight
strike on the gates of hell. He would
throw off his torpor sometimes
to help the hangman in his work.
When his eyes held a gleam
it was a spark from fires he lit
for burning heretics.
He was an enemy to thought, mankind,
to life, to progress, righteousness,
faithful to Rome: King Satan
reigning in the name of Christ.
In his dark mind plots hissed sliding
like serpents. Light never touched
the gloomy ceilings of his palaces:
no feasts, no courtesy, no clowns –
for play betrayal and for diversion
torture. All other kings
felt in the dark his projects over them,
half grasped. His thought
pressed on the universe. He had
the power, the will for conquest,
dissolution. At prayer his voice
fell like a thunderbolt, zigzags
of lightning issued from his dreams.
Those he was merely thinking of said,
'I can't breathe.' The nations under him
shuddered beneath the sleepless
fire of his gaze.
Charles was the vulture but his son,
Philip, broods now
stealthy and furtive as an owl:
black doublet,
the Golden Fleece about his neck,
bleak, unmoving, the cold

sentinel of destiny whose eye
gleams like the one pale chink
letting air into a cellar.
Now, all alone, he moves one finger
seeming to trace an order to the dark.
Unprecedented then a bitter smile
winces across his lips.
He sees his army on the sea
growing in might and moved by his design.
He stands
on the pinnacle of time and watches.
All goes well. The ocean's smooth.
The armada calms it as the Ark the Flood.
The fleet is in good order and the ships
keeping to their fixed pattern
form a vast grid upon the sea, chessboard
of decks and spindrift, and the masts
sway with their rigging.
His vessels are sacred and the waves
make way for them, reefs
disappear, currents
perform their duty as they lovingly
speed the hulls forward, each man-of-war
under its boatswain –
fierce Portuguese, sailors from Flanders,
men from the Pyrenean rivers,
soldiers, captains, generals –
on ships from Germany, from Naples,
galleons from Cadiz.
And Philip bends
over the vast armada hearing
the cries, mouths cupped in hands,
all making ready for the fight –
pounding of feet along the bulwarks,
orders from the admiral with his hand
on the shipboy's shoulder,
sea-signals, sound of drums,
shrill whistles and the sinister
command to clear the decks.
Sails beat like wings

above these citadels of wood.
The sea thunders as the fleet
moves on resounding to its goal
and the baleful king smiles counting
four hundred ships and eighty thousand swords.
His lips form a vampire's snarl
greedy for blood. Philip holds England.
Who can save her now? One flame
touched to the powder and the lightning strikes.
The king has storm clouds clustered in his grasp.
None can withstand his thunderbolts when they're unleashed.
He is the lord who cannot be gainsaid.
He's the true heir of Caesar, he's the king
whose shadow falls on half the globe.
All's finished once he says, 'I want.'
He grips his victory by the hair.
He launched the fleet and now the sea
is dutiful. These winged black ships,
this countless swarm of dragons – he alone
set them in movement with one push
from his little finger. He's the king,
the dark commander of the vastest fleet
the world has ever seen.
When Béit-Cifresil had dug the well
for the Great Mosque at Cairo
he carved this phrase:
'The heavens may be God's. I have the earth.'
All tyrants merge in history into one
so what the sultan uttered once
is the monarch's thought today. The world
is his.

In silence by the pool meanwhile
the Infanta holds her rose,
unsmiling now.
                    A sudden breeze
thrown by the evening across the plain
brushes the skyline ruffling
the surface of the stream. Reeds
tremble and the clumps of trees

sway shuddering.
The breeze arrives and takes the rose,
strips it of all its petals sending them,
random, over the pool.
The Infanta's hand now holds
an empty stalk. She bends
over the water, sees
the ruin of the flower and cannot
understand. She is afraid
and glances in amazement at the sky
trying to find this wind
that did not seem to mind displeasing her.
The pool was bright before but now
seethes with dark waves.
The poor rose is dispersed
and the hundred scattered petals start to sink,
tossed by the ripples, waterlogged,
sent by the wind now here, now there,
drowning.
'My lady,' the duenna says, her face in shadow,
'Everything on earth belongs to princes
'save the wind.'

23 May 1859

After the Battle

My father was a hero though his smile
was gentle and it chanced one evening while
attended by his best hussar, a man
of strength and courage, he rode out to scan
the field strewn with the dead on whom the night
was falling. Then he thought he heard a slight
sound in the shadows. There, abandoned by
the fleeing Spanish troops, a soldier, dry-
throated, pale, bleeding, crawled on the road's brink,
and more than half-dead cried again, 'A drink
for pity's sake!' My father took the flask
of brandy off his saddle, turned to ask
his aide to hand it over. Suddenly,
as soon as the hussar bent down to see
to him, the soldier, some kind of a Moor,
lifted the pistol he was clutching, swore
an oath, took rapid aim and fired straight at
my father so the bullet struck his hat
making his horse shy back, tossing its head.
'Go on. Give him a drink,' my father said.

18 June 1850

Orders for the Day: Late Spring

The victory is ours! And so
    first thing today
I'm dashing off this fresh
    communiqué.

On hills let the trumpet
    peal loud and long –
the fight for the lilac's
    been won by the spring.

Girls' toes needn't shiver
    entering the shoe –
warmth stirs in the sky's
    immensity of blue.

Birds sing and lambs are grazing.
    May, with jeers,
keeps firing as winter retreats
    riddled with flowers.

Rosa's Angry

They're quarrelling. Why?
   Because they adore
each other. (When I
   say 'Darling' be sure
      I'll soon be needing
      terms less misleading.)

You try to untie
   the bonds round the heart.
The sun leaves the sky
   and heavy clouds start
      forming above a
      changeable lover.

The weather looks clear,
   the birds sing in tune.
You stroll without fear
   through woods gold with June –
      brilliance of morning
      offers no warning.

But later you may
   be caught in a shower
for any fine day
   can change in an hour –
      and who can foretell
      the end of a spell?

The Sower

It is the evening moment.
    Quiet, by the farmhouse door,
I see the sun's glow lighting
    Labour's last hour.

On fields now drowned by nightfall
    In rags one old man sows
The gold of next year's harvest
    Into the rows.

His tall form, black now, moving
    Over the soil displays
His deep faith in the useful
    Passage of days.

He paces slowly, throwing
    The fine handfuls of grain,
Goes back and forth unceasing.
    I watch unseen.

The dark is spreading over
    The sounds that come from far.
The sower's hand now reaches
    The highest star.

'The children read . . .'

The children read, blond heads
bowed, spelling out the words,
and their teacher
scolds them, spring light all around.
I can see the half-open
windows of the school
as I stroll in the water-meadows
and the green season,
immense,
shivers through the distant forest.

There's laughter everywhere. And song.
It's like a universe
on holiday. Each blossom seems
created of sheer rays of light.
I pore over these joyous pages
spelling out the words –
each blue flower makes a line of verse
and the eagle describes the curve
of a stanza with its wing.

All is not clear though as I read.
Nothing
is quite without stain.
What are the links between
a lily, a pure lily,
and the perverseness of these thistles?
A blackbird sings. A teal
breaks from the reeds with drops
of water falling from its bill
like tears of death,
hurt pearls.
       The fish it's caught
pursued that spider scuttling
over its vague blue home, the strange
transparent world of water. I hear

a sudden gunshot from the wood
and dogs barking.
                    There's
a wound among this wonder.
My footsteps print damp ground
below this grass. A sad
newcomer among this beauty,
I think about evil – that enigma –
that spelling-mistake God made.

23 October 1859

Onset of Winter

Go away! said the north wind,
It's my turn to sing.
And trembling,
surprised by the anger
in the command,
not daring
to linger,
disconcerted, my songs
have been kicked out
by the bullying cold.

Rain. They send me away
whatever I try
to do, all my songs
are the wrong ones.
The comedy's over.
I call to the swallows –
Time we were off.

Hailstones. Wind.
The scraggy branches
twist in the trees.
In the distance the smoke
hurries white
over a grey sky.

Last pallor of gold
lies on the cold slopes.
The air through the keyhole
blows on my hand.

During an Illness

They say I'm very ill. My eyes
are tarnished over. The bone
finger of the infinite
taps on my shoulder.

I get up only to fall
back into bed. There's a taste
of earth in my mouth.
The air I breathe smells foul.

I shiver like a boat's sail
at the harbour-bar. I move slowly.
It's cold. Under this white sheet
my body's stretched like a corpse.

Nothing warms these hands.
My flesh sweats like melting snow.
I feel a draught on my temples
blowing from far away.

Is it the wind of darkness –
the wind that passed by Christ?
Is it the grand Nothing of Lucretius?
Or Spinoza's All?

Doctors seem gloomy as they leave me.
Visitors lower their voices.
Things lean over me
looking scared.

I hear the murmur, 'He's done for.'
My body shakes. The armour
of my mind is coming apart
nail by nail.

That vast final moment
is on its way through the dark.
A distant gleam shows where a star
is rising in a wan sky.

Time – reality or fraud –
lifts its puzzling brow.
I gaze unflinching, eager
to sound the secret at last.

My soul narrows down to an eye
plumbing the depths of God.
I grope at the gates of eternity
trying my key in the night.

Grave-diggers scoop out the shape
of God. Dying will be to know.
Death is showing me to my seat.
I've come to see his black show.

3 October 1859

For Jeanne, Ill During the Siege of Paris

I keep watch on my knees by your bed,
      pray for my death to be close,
yours far away – but if the tally
      of our days has got confused,

If you continue to look so pale
      in this stifling air of ours,
If I see my old man's dark shadow
      falling on you, my grandchild,

If your hands stay so frail they appear
      transparent, if shivering there
In your cot you look like a fledgling
      waiting for your wings to grow,

If you don't seem to want to take root
      for long in this earth of ours,
If your eyes wander in displeasure
      over the mysteries of life,

If you aren't gay, rosy-cheeked and strong,
      If you keep having sad dreams,
If you won't turn and shut behind you
      the door through which you entered,

If I don't see you walking upright
      straight-backed like a beautiful
woman, laughing, and it seems your soul
      does not wish to abide here –

Then in this world where shrouds can sometimes
      be found next to swaddling-clothes
I'll think you are the angel whose task
      it is to take me away.

Whose Fault Is It?

'You've just burned down the Library?'
                                        'Yes. I
started the fire.'
                    'But that's an appalling crime,
a crime committed against yourself.
You've just destroyed the light of your own mind,
blown out the torch that guided you.
Your senseless act of sacrilege has burned
what's yours, your treasure,
your fortune, your inheritance.
Books are on your side against the masters.
Books have always been your defence.
A library's an act of faith
that generations make inside the dark
as testimony of the eventual dawn.
And now you've put a lighted torch to that
sacred collection of truths,
to those masterworks of thunder and brightness,
to time's graveyard that becomes
a storehouse, to the work of centuries,
to ancient man, to history, to the past
(which is a lesson for the future to spell out),
to what was begun so as never to end,
to poetry, to the depths within a Bible,
to that hallowed pile where the works
of Aeschylus, where Homer, where the Book of Job
stand on the horizon,
to Molière, Voltaire and Kant,
to the establishment of reason – you've set
a lighted torch to those,
reduced the human mind to smoke
forgetting that it's books
that rescue you from oppression.
Books are set on a hill. They shine.
And because they shed light on wars
and famine and the scaffold they destroy them.
When books speak out then slaves

and outcasts are no more. Open a book –
read Plato, Milton, Beccaria,
read the prophets, Dante, Shakespeare, Corneille –
the immensities of soul that they possess
awake in you. Dazzled you feel
like them. In reading you become
pensive and grave and gentle.
The grandeur of these men
grows in your spirit and you feel
them teaching you the way a dawn
illuminates some cloister. The deeper
their hot light plunges in your heart
the more you feel at peace,
the more you feel alive. They question your soul
and you're prepared to answer.
You realize you're good, then better.
Your pride, your anger,
evil, prejudices,
kings, emperors melt
like snow at the fire, since man first
gains knowledge and only then his liberty.
And all this light is yours,
belongs to you, is yours by right –
do you understand? – and you're
the one who put it out.
Books have already reached the goals you dream of.
They get inside your thought unloosing
the bonds that error places round the truth –
for knowledge is always tied with intricate knots.
Books are your doctors, guides and guardians.
They cure your hatred, take insanity away.
It's your fault that you've lost all this.
Books are the wealth that belongs to you,
they're knowledge and truth and justice,
they're virtue, duty, progress,
reason that dissipates all frenzy –
that is what you've destroyed.'
                                    'But I can't read.'

June 1871

142

To Théophile Gautier

Friend, poet, fleeing our black night, you've left
the region of our noise to enter glory
and now your name will blaze on those pure hills.
I knew you young and handsome, loved you well –
and more than once in our proud flights together
your loyal wings supported my distraction.
Now that the days fall white on me like snow
I recollect times past, and looking back
on those lost years that saw our two suns rise,
on struggles, tempests, shouts in the arena,
on new art opening as men cried out, Yes –
I hear those marvellous winds that blow no longer.

You took your heritage from ancient Greece
as well as younger France and while you paid
proud homage to the dead with words of hope
you never closed your eyes towards tomorrow.
Working with skill inside your secret forge
you'd twist all rays into one single flame.
At ease with Patroclus and Oliver,
as seer at Thebes or by the druid's stone,
as priest in Rome or India, you'd place
an angel's arrow in each god's curved bow.
In you the sunset met the dawn, in your
inventive brain the future crossed the past.
You crowned age-old tradition with new art.
You knew that when an unfamiliar voice
speaks from a whirl of lightning in the clouds
it must be heard and taken to the heart.
Calmly you scorned the vile attempts of all
who spat at Aeschylus and mocked at Shakespeare.
You knew our age had its own air to breathe,
that art progresses by transfiguring,
that beauty is embellished when it's joined
with what is great. You showed your real joy
when drama seized on Paris as its prey,
when age-old frosts were hunted by the spring,

when unforeseen the star of modern thought
set sudden fire to the sky and when
the Hippogriff took on from Pegasus!

I greet you on the grim threshold of death.
Seek the truth now for you discovered beauty.
Climb that harsh stairway. From the top you'll see
a black bridge arching over the abyss.
Die – for the final hour's the final step.
You'll find those chasms please your eagle-heart,
you'll see the absolute, the real, sublime,
and feel the wild wind blowing round those peaks
in all the dazzle of eternity.
You'll look down on Olympus from the heights
of heaven and you'll see all human dreams
for what they are – Job's dreams as well as Homer's.
You'll see Jehovah from the heights of God.
Climb then and grow, spread out your wings and soar!

Each time a living being leaves us I
watch moved – for death's a temple all must enter
and when a man dies I can clearly see
the moment of my own ascent approaching.
I feel, my friend, the dark sum of my days.
I have begun my death by solitude.
Depths of my evening glimmer now with stars.
It's time for me as well to take my leave.
My long life's thread is near the fatal blade.
The wind which carried you away lifts me.
I'll follow those who loved me, though proscribed:
their gaze attracts me to infinity.
I'm coming – do not close the gates of death.

Let us pass through. None can elude that law.
All's in decline – this vivid century
is entering immenser shadows where
we scurry, pale, for those great noons are gone.
Hear through the twilight that wild noise as oaks
are felled to make a pyre for Hercules.
The steeds of death begin to neigh for joy

because a brilliant age draws to its close.
This haughty century that tamed the gale
is dying – Gautier, their peer and brother,
follows Dumas, Musset and Lamartine.
The ancient springs reviving us have dried.
No more is there a river Styx, no more
is there a fountain of eternal youth.
The dour reaper with his scythe comes step
by step towards what's left now of the corn.
It's my turn soon. Night fills my troubled eyes
and guessing sadly what the future holds
for my dear grandchildren, two threatened doves,
their father dead, I standing here alone
weep over cradles smiling at the grave.

2 November 1872. All Souls' Day

Orpheus

I call on the god of the six black springs
that feed this river.
I call on Zeus who commands the thundering
ox-drawn chariot of his mother Rhea
and the silent chariot of Night
brought by the dark-winged horses.
I call on the vanished giants
and the new race of men.
I call on the gods of ending and creation,
on gods of the underworld and of the sky.
Let them all listen.
      I adore
a mortal woman.
      Far out to sea,
Poseidon, the monster with blue hair,
can hear me. Answer my prayer!
I am the human soul in song
in love.
    The halls of darkness fill
with clouds, rain crashes
on the seething leaves.
The north wind stirs the wood, the west
the fields of wheat. Thus
are our hearts moved with love.
I'll worship her, Eurydice,
forever, anywhere! If I should fail,
may heaven curse me, curse
the flower in bloom, the ripened ear of corn!
Do not write magic words upon the wall.

3 February 1877

After the Caudine Forks

Rome was too proud, the gods
punished her, the Samnites
had the triumph
of a coward's victory.
Those of us still alive knew
mourning in those days.
Nothing prevents the dawn
from blossoming gold
above these hills.
Out near the paupers' graveyard there's
a race-course where I go
sometimes, keep a vague eye
on what is going on,
the crowd, the thronging
to and fro. The field
leads to barracks where the troops
come and go as though in a city
still under siege.
It's April now, the weather
smiles, birds sing. Far off,
beyond the slopes where morning
starts to glow and where
wild roses disclose their petals,
the trumpets whisper
distant news of doom
and I listen, moved.
I was there today. Clouds sometimes
are able to restrain the sky.
The sun grew overcast.
Abruptly, mounted,
lance in hand, a troop
of weather-beaten veterans passed
like soldiers from the age of heroes.
Little children
ran up and followed them.
Ahead, three horsemen, one
after the other, put

a bugle to their lips and blew
a fanfare so the sound
martial and lucid
rang without a pause for breath,
and, splendid, on they rode
over the plain, unhurried,
ageless. Their shields
glittered with carved Medusas so the foe
would turn to stone. Plumes
on their helmets tossed
proudly in the wind as if lions
were shaking their manes.
As they cantered past you felt
their polished metal should only catch
the light of sunrise. Girls agreed
how fine they were and all
was joy, flowers
sweetened the hedges, passers-by
looked happy and the sky
was gilded but
remembering these were defeated men
I found my eyes
were filled with tears.

Open Windows: Early Morning

Voices. Light through my eyelids. Bells lurch
into action at St Peter's Church.
Bathers shouting. 'This way!' Others yell,
'No! Over here!' Birds are prattling. Jeanne as well.
Georges calls her. Cocks crowing. Up on the roof
scrape of a trowel. Knocking. Outside, a hoof
clatters. Someone's using a scythe in long grass.
Dull sounds. They're fixing tiles above my head.
The harbour's din. Hot machines start to hiss.
A brass band on the wind now faint now loud.
Uproar from the quayside. French voices. 'Bonjour.
'Merci. Au revoir.' It must be late now for
the robin's taken up his song.
In the forge an anvil begins to ring.
Water lapping on stone. A steamer hoots. A fly
buzzes in. And still the sea's vast sigh.

Grand-daughter

Jeanne squatting on the grass looked pensive,
a serious curve to her pink cheek.
I went up. 'Anything you want?'
For I obey my grandchildren, observe them,
try all the time to grasp what's in their head.
And she replied. 'Beasties.'
So I parted grass-blades, found an ant.
'There you are.' She was half-satisfied.
'No, beasties are big,' she told me.
                                    They dream
the huge. Seas lure them to the shore,
lull them with a harsh rhythm,
enticing them with shadow
and the monstrous flying of the wind.
They relish terror, need the marvellous.
I had no elephant handy and apologized.
'Won't something else do? Tell me, Jeanne.'
She raised a tiny finger at the sky.
'That,' she said. It was time for evening.
I saw the moon's great disc on the horizon.

To My Daughter Adèle

You slept near me as a baby
fresh and rosy as the Christ-child
in the cradle and your slumber
was so tranquil that you never
heard the bird sing in the shadow
while I breathed the sombre beauty
falling from the vault of heaven
      as I thought about you.

Listening to the angels flying
overhead I watched you sleeping
and I'd scatter in the silence
jasmine petals on your bed-clothes
keeping guard above your eyelids
closed in sleep and say my prayers
weeping when I thought of all that
      waits for us in the night.

One day soon it will be my turn
sleeping on a bed of shadow
in a room so bleak and silent
I shan't hear the bird sing either.
When the night is black around me –
then your tears, your prayer, your flowers
will, my dove, repay my coffin
      what I once gave your crib.

4 October 1857

The French texts

Au vallon de Cherizy

*Factus sum peregrinus . . . et quaesivi qui simul
contristaretur, et non fuit.* Ps. LXVIII

Perfice gressus meos semitis tuis. Ps. XVI

*Je suis devenu voyageur . . . et j'ai cherché qui
s'affligerait avec moi, et nul n'est venu.
Permets à mes pas de suivre ta trace.*

Le voyageur s'assied sous votre ombre immobile,
Beau vallon; triste et seul, il contemple en rêvant
L'oiseau qui fuit l'oiseau, l'eau que souille un reptile,
    Et le jonc qu'agite le vent!

Hélas! l'homme fuit l'homme; et souvent avant l'âge
Dans un cœur noble et pur se glisse le malheur;
Heureux l'humble roseau qu'alors un prompt orage
    En passant brise dans sa fleur!

Cet orage, ô vallon, le voyageur l'implore.
Déjà las de sa course, il est bien loin encore
    Du terme où ses maux vont finir;
Il voit devant ses pas, seul pour se soutenir,
Aux rayons nébuleux de sa funèbre aurore,
    Le grand désert de l'avenir!

De dégoûts en dégoûts il va traîner sa vie.
Que lui font ces faux biens qu'un faux orgueil envie?
Il cherche un cœur fidèle, ami de ses douleurs;
Mais en vain: nuls secours n'aplaniront sa voie,
Nul parmi les mortels ne rira de sa joie,
    Nul ne pleurera de ses pleurs!

Son sort est l'abandon; et sa vie isolée
Ressemble au noir cyprès qui croît dans la vallée.
Loin de lui, le lys vierge ouvre au jour son bouton;
Et jamais, égayant son ombre malheureuse,
    Une jeune vigne amoureuse
A ses sombres rameaux n'enlace un vert feston.

    Avant de gravir la montagne,
Un moment au vallon le voyageur a fui.
Le silence du moins répond à son ennui.
Il est seul dans la foule: ici, douce compagne,
    La solitude est avec lui!

Isolés comme lui, mais plus que lui tranquilles,
Arbres, gazons, riants asiles,
Sauvez ce malheureux du regard des humains!
Ruisseaux, livrez vos bords, ouvrez vos flots dociles
A ses pieds qu'a souillés la fange de leurs villes,
Et la poudre de leurs chemins!

Ah! laissez-lui chanter, consolé sous vos ombres,
Ce long songe idéal de nos jours les plus sombres,
La vierge au front si pur, au sourire si beau!
Si pour l'hymen d'un jour c'est en vain qu'il l'appelle,
Laissez du moins rêver à son âme immortelle
L'éternel hymen du tombeau!

La terre ne tient point sa pensée asservie;
Le bel espoir l'enlève au triste souvenir;
Deux ombres désormais dominent sur sa vie:
L'une est dans le passé, l'autre dans l'avenir!

Oh! dis, quand viendras-tu? quel Dieu va te conduire,
Etre charmant et doux, vers celui que tu plains?
Astre ami, quand viendras-tu luire,
Comme un soleil nouveau, sur ses jours orphelins?

Il ne t'obtiendra point, chère et noble conquête,
Au prix de ces vertus qu'il ne peut oublier;
Il laisse au gré du vent le jonc courber sa tête;
Il sera le grand chêne, et devant la tempête
Il saura rompre et non plier.

Elle approche, il la voit; mais il la voit sans crainte.
Adieu, flots purs, berceaux épais,
Beau vallon où l'on trouve un écho pour sa plainte,
Bois heureux où l'on souffre en paix!

Heureux qui peut au sein du vallon solitaire,
Naître, vivre et mourir dans le champ paternel!
Il ne connaît rien de la terre,
Et ne voit jamais que le ciel!

Juillet 1821

Le matin

Moriturus morituræ!

Le voile du matin sur les monts se déploie.
Vois, un rayon naissant blanchit la vieille tour;
Et déjà dans les cieux s'unit avec amour,
    Ainsi que la gloire à la joie,
Le premier chant des bois aux premiers feux du jour.

Oui, souris à l'éclat dont le ciel se décore! –
Tu verras, si demain le cercueil me dévore,
Luire à tes yeux en pleurs un soleil aussi beau,
Et les mêmes oiseaux chanter la même aurore,
    Sur mon noir et muet tombeau!

Mais dans l'autre horizon l'âme alors est ravie.
L'avenir sans fin s'ouvre à l'être illimité.
    Au matin de l'éternité,
    On se réveille de la vie,
Comme d'une nuit sombre ou d'un rêve agité!

Avril 1822

L'enfant

O horror! horror! horror! – Shakespeare, *Macbeth*

Les Turcs ont passé là: tout est ruine et deuil.
Chio, l'île des vins, n'est plus qu'un sombre écueil,
    Chio, qu'ombrageaient les charmilles,
Chio, qui dans les flots reflétait ses grands bois,
Ses coteaux, ses palais, et le soir quelquefois
    Un chœur dansant de jeunes filles.

Tout est désert: mais non, seul près des murs noircis,
Un enfant aux yeux bleus, un enfant grec, assis,
    Courbait sa tête humiliée.
Il avait pour asile, il avait pour appui
Une blanche aubépine, une fleur, comme lui
    Dans le grand ravage oubliée.

– Ah! pauvre enfant, pieds nus sur les rocs anguleux!
Hélas! pour essuyer les pleurs de tes yeux bleus
      Comme le ciel et comme l'onde,
Pour que dans leur azur, de larmes orageux,
Passe le vif éclair de la joie et des jeux,
      Pour relever ta tête blonde,

Que veux-tu? bel enfant, que te faut-il donner
Pour rattacher gaîment et gaîment ramener
      En boucles sur ta blanche épaule
Ces cheveux, qui du fer n'ont pas subi l'affront,
Et qui pleurent épars autour de ton beau front,
      Comme les feuilles sur le saule?

Qui pourrait dissiper tes chagrins nébuleux?
Est-ce d'avoir ce lis, bleu comme tes yeux bleus,
      Qui d'Iran borde le puits sombre?
Ou le fruit du tuba, de cet arbre si grand
Qu'un cheval au galop met toujours en courant
      Cent ans à sortir de son ombre?

Veux-tu, pour me sourire, un bel oiseau des bois,
Qui chante avec un chant plus doux que le hautbois,
      Plus éclatant que les cymbales?
Que veux-tu? fleur, beau fruit ou l'oiseau merveilleux?
– Ami, dit l'enfant grec, dit l'enfant aux yeux bleus,
      Je veux de la poudre et des balles.

Juin 1828

Attente

Esperaba, desperada.

Monte, écureuil, monte au grand chêne,
Sur la branche des cieux prochaine,
Qui plie et tremble comme un jonc.
Cigogne, aux vieilles tours fidèle,
Oh! vole, et monte à tire-d'aile
De l'église à la citadelle,
Du haut clocher au grand donjon.

[*pp.* 31–33]

Vieux aigle, monte de ton aire
A la montagne centenaire
Que blanchit l'hiver éternel;
Et toi qu'en ta couche inquiète
Jamais l'aube ne vit muette,
Monte, monte, vive alouette,
Vive alouette, monte au ciel!

Et maintenant, du haut de l'arbre,
Des flèches de la tour de marbre,
Du grand mont, du ciel enflammé,
A l'horizon, parmi la brume,
Voyez-vous flotter une plume,
Et courir un cheval qui fume,
Et revenir mon bien-aimé?

Juin 1828

Rêverie

> *Lo giorno se n'andava, e l'aer bruno*
> *Toglieva gli animai che sono'n terra*
> *Dalle fatiche loro.*   DANTE

Oh! laissez-moi! c'est l'heure où l'horizon qui fume
Cache un front inégal sous un cercle de brume;
L'heure où l'astre géant rougit et disparaît.
Le grand bois jaunissant dore seul la colline.
On dirait qu'en ces jours où l'automne décline,
Le soleil et la pluie ont rouillé la forêt.

Oh! qui fera surgir soudain, qui fera naître,
Là-bas, – tandis que seul je rêve à la fenêtre
Et que l'ombre s'amasse au fond du corridor, –
Quelque ville mauresque, éclatante, inouïe,
Qui, comme la fusée en gerbe épanouie,
Déchire ce brouillard avec ses flèches d'or!

Qu'elle vienne inspirer, ranimer, ô génies!
Mes chansons, comme un ciel d'automne rembrunies,
Et jeter dans mes yeux son magique reflet,
Et longtemps, s'éteignant en rumeurs étouffées,
Avec les mille tours de ses palais de fées,
Brumeuse, denteler l'horizon violet!

Septembre 1828

Soleils couchants, VI

Le soleil s'est couché ce soir dans les nuées;
Demain viendra l'orage, et le soir, et la nuit;
Puis l'aube, et ses clartés de vapeurs obstruées;
Puis les nuits, puis les jours, pas du temps qui s'enfuit!

Tous ces jours passeront; ils passeront en foule
Sur la face des mers, sur la face des monts,
Sur les fleuves d'argent, sur les forêts où roule
Comme un hymne confus des morts que nous aimons.

Et la face des eaux, et le front des montagnes,
Ridés et non vieillis, et les bois toujours verts
S'iront rajeunissant; le fleuve des campagnes
Prendra sans cesse aux monts le flot qu'il donne aux mers.

Mais moi, sous chaque jour courbant plus bas ma tête,
Je passe, et, refroidi sous ce soleil joyeux,
Je m'en irai bientôt, au milieu de la fête,
Sans que rien manque au monde, immense et radieux!

22 avril 1829

A un voyageur

*L'une partie du monde ne sait point comme l'autre
vit et se gouverne.* PHILIPPE DE COMMINES

Ami, vous revenez d'un de ces longs voyages
Qui nous font vieillir vite, et nous changent en sages
      Au sortir du berceau.
De tous les océans votre course a vu l'onde,
Hélas! et vous feriez une ceinture au monde
      Du sillon du vaisseau.

Le soleil de vingt cieux a mûri votre vie.
Partout où vous mena votre inconstante envie,
      Jetant et ramassant,
Pareil au laboureur qui récolte et qui sème,
Vous avez pris des lieux et laissé de vous-même
      Quelque chose en passant.

Tandis que votre ami, moins heureux et moins sage,
Attendait des saisons l'uniforme passage
  Dans le même horizon,
Et comme l'arbre vert qui de loin la dessine,
A sa porte effeuillant ses jours, prenait racine
  Au seuil de sa maison!

Vous êtes fatigué, tant vous avez vu d'hommes!
Enfin vous revenez, las de ce que nous sommes,
  Vous reposer en Dieu.
Triste, vous me contez vos courses infécondes,
Et vos pieds ont mêlé la poudre de trois mondes
  Aux cendres de mon feu.

Or, maintenant, le cœur plein de choses profondes,
Des enfants dans vos mains tenant les têtes blondes,
  Vous me parlez ici,
Et vous me demandez, sollicitude amère!
– Où donc ton père? où donc ton fils? où donc ta mère?
  – Ils voyagent aussi!

Le voyage qu'ils font n'a ni soleil, ni lune;
Nul homme n'y peut rien porter de sa fortune,
  Tant le maître est jaloux!
Le voyage qu'ils font est profond et sans bornes,
On le fait à pas lents, parmi des faces mornes,
  Et nous le ferons tous!

J'étais à leur départ comme j'étais au vôtre.
En diverses saisons, tous trois, l'un après l'autre,
  Ils ont pris leur essor.
Hélas! j'ai mis en terre, à cette heure suprême,
Ces têtes que j'aimais. Avare, j'ai moi-même
  Enfoui mon trésor.

Je les ai vus partir. J'ai, faible et plein d'alarmes,
Vu trois fois un drap noir semé de blanches larmes
  Tendre ce corridor.
J'ai sur leurs froides mains pleuré comme une femme.
Mais, le cercueil fermé, mon âme a vu leur âme
  Ouvrir deux ailes d'or!

Je les ai vus partir comme trois hirondelles
Qui vont chercher bien loin des printemps plus fidèles
  Et des étés meilleurs.
Ma mère vit le ciel, et partit la première,
Et son œil en mourant fut plein d'une lumière
  Qu'on n'a point vue ailleurs.

Et puis mon premier-né la suivit; puis mon père,
Fier vétéran âgé de quarante ans de guerre,
    Tout chargé de chevrons.
Maintenant ils sont là! tous trois dorment dans l'ombre,
Tandis que leurs esprits font le voyage sombre,
    Et vont où nous irons!

Si vous voulez, à l'heure où la lune décline,
Nous monterons tous deux la nuit sur la colline
    Où gisent nos aïeux.
Je vous dirai, montrant à votre vue amie
La ville morte auprès de la ville endormie:
    Laquelle dort le mieux?

Venez; muets tous deux et couchés contre terre,
Nous entendrons, tandis que Paris fera taire
    Son vivant tourbillon,
Ces millions de morts, moisson du fils de l'homme,
Sourdre confusément dans leurs sépulcres, comme
    Le grain dans le sillon!

Combien vivent joyeux qui devaient, sœurs ou frères,
Faire un pleur éternel de quelques ombres chères!
    Pouvoir des ans vainqueurs!
Les morts durent bien peu. Laissons-les sous la pierre!
Hélas! dans le cercueil ils tombent en poussière
    Moins vite qu'en nos cœurs!

Voyageur! voyageur! Quelle est notre folie!
Qui sait combien de morts à chaque heure on oublie?
    Des plus chers, des plus beaux?
Qui peut savoir combien toute douleur s'émousse,
Et combien sur la terre un jour d'herbe qui pousse
    Efface de tombeaux!

6 juillet 1829

        [pp. 37–38]

'Lorsque l'enfant paraît . . .'

Le toit s'égaie et rit – A<small>NDRÉ</small> C<small>HÉNIER</small>

Lorsque l'enfant paraît, le cercle de famille
Applaudit à grands cris. Son doux regard qui brille
      Fait briller tous les yeux,
Et les plus tristes fronts, les plus souillés peut-être,
Se dérident soudain à voir l'enfant paraître,
      Innocent et joyeux.

Soit que juin ait verdi mon seuil, ou que novembre
Fasse autour d'un grand feu vacillant dans la chambre
      Les chaises se toucher,
Quand l'enfant vient, la joie arrive et nous éclaire.
On rit, on se récrie, on l'appelle, et sa mère
      Tremble à le voir marcher.

Quelquefois nous parlons, en remuant la flamme,
De patrie et de Dieu, des poètes, de l'âme
      Qui s'élève en priant;
L'enfant paraît, adieu le ciel et la patrie
Et les poètes saints! la grave causerie
      S'arrête en souriant.

La nuit, quand l'homme dort, quand l'esprit rêve, à l'heure
Où l'on entend gémir, comme une voix qui pleure,
      L'onde entre les roseaux,
Si l'aube tout à coup là-bas luit comme un phare,
Sa clarté dans les champs éveille une fanfare
      De cloches et d'oiseaux!

Enfant, vous êtes l'aube et mon âme est la plaine
Qui des plus douces fleurs embaume son haleine
      Quand vous la respirez;
Mon âme est la forêt dont les sombres ramures
S'emplissent pour vous seul de suaves murmures
      Et de rayons dorés!

Car vos beaux yeux sont pleins de douceurs infinies,
Car vos petites mains, joyeuses et bénies,
      N'ont point mal fait encor;
Jamais vos jeunes pas n'ont touché notre fange,
Tête sacrée! enfant aux cheveux blonds! bel ange
      A l'auréole d'or!

Vous êtes parmi nous la colombe de l'arche.
Vos pieds tendres et purs n'ont point l'âge où l'on marche;
      Vos ailes sont d'azur.
Sans le comprendre encor vous regardez le monde.
Double virginité! corps où rien n'est immonde,
      Ame où rien n'est impur!

Il est si beau, l'enfant, avec son doux sourire,
Sa douce bonne foi, sa voix qui veut tout dire,
      Ses pleurs vite apaisés,
Laissant errer sa vue étonnée et ravie,
Offrant de toutes parts sa jeune âme à la vie
      Et sa bouche aux baisers!

Seigneur! préservez-moi, préservez ceux que j'aime,
Frères, parents, amis, et mes ennemis même
      Dans le mal triomphants,
De jamais voir, Seigneur! l'été sans fleurs vermeilles,
La cage sans oiseaux, la ruche sans abeilles,
      La maison sans enfants!

18 mai 1830

'Oh! qui que vous soyez . . .'

Quien no ama, no vive.

Oh! qui que vous soyez, jeune ou vieux, riche ou sage,
Si jamais vous n'avez épié le passage,
Le soir, d'un pas léger, d'un pas mélodieux,
D'un voile blanc qui glisse et fuit dans les ténèbres,
Et, comme un météore au sein des nuits funèbres,
Vous laisse dans le cœur un sillon radieux;

Si vous ne connaissez que pour l'entendre dire
Au poète amoureux qui chante et qui soupire,
Ce suprême bonheur qui fait nos jours dorés,
De posséder un cœur sans réserve et sans voiles,
De n'avoir pour flambeaux, de n'avoir pour étoiles,
De n'avoir pour soleils que deux yeux adorés;

Si vous n'avez jamais attendu, morne et sombre,
Sous les vitres d'un bal qui rayonne dans l'ombre,

[*pp.* 40–42]

L'heure où pour le départ les portes s'ouvriront,
Pour voir votre beauté, comme un éclair qui brille,
Rose avec des yeux bleus et toute jeune fille,
Passer dans la lumière avec des fleurs au front;

Si vous n'avez jamais senti la frénésie
De voir la main qu'on veut par d'autres mains choisie,
De voir le cœur aimé battre sur d'autres cœurs;
Si vous n'avez jamais vu d'un œil de colère
La valse impure, au vol lascif et circulaire,
Effeuiller en courant les femmes et les fleurs;

Si jamais vous n'avez descendu les collines,
Le cœur tout débordant d'émotions divines;
Si jamais vous n'avez, le soir, sous les tilleuls,
Tandis qu'au ciel luisaient des étoiles sans nombre,
Aspiré, couple heureux, la volupté de l'ombre,
Cachés, et vous parlant tout bas, quoique tout seuls;

Si jamais une main n'a fait trembler la vôtre;
Si jamais ce seul mot qu'on dit l'un après l'autre,
Je t'aime! n'a rempli votre âme tout un jour;
Si jamais vous n'avez pris en pitié les trônes
En songeant qu'on cherchait les sceptres, les couronnes,
Et la gloire, et l'empire, et qu'on avait l'amour!

La nuit, quand la veilleuse agonise dans l'urne,
Quand Paris, enfoui sous la brume nocturne
Avec la tour saxonne et l'église des Goths,
Laisse sans les compter passer les heures noires
Qui, douze fois, semant les rêves illusoires,
S'envolent des clochers par groupes inégaux;

Si jamais vous n'avez, à l'heure où tout sommeille,
Tandis qu'elle dormait, oublieuse et vermeille,
Pleuré comme un enfant à force de souffrir,
Crié cent fois son nom du soir jusqu'à l'aurore,
Et cru qu'elle viendrait en l'appelant encore,
Et maudit votre mère, et désiré mourir;

Si jamais vous n'avez senti que d'une femme
Le regard dans votre âme allumait une autre âme,
Que vous étiez charmé, qu'un ciel s'était ouvert,
Et que pour cette enfant, qui de vos pleurs se joue,
Il vous serait bien doux, d'expirer sur la roue;...
Vous n'avez point aimé, vous n'avez point souffert!

Novembre 1831

Napoléon II (*extrait*)

Oh! demain, c'est la grande chose!
De quoi demain sera-t-il fait?
L'homme aujourd'hui sème le cause,
Demain Dieu fait mûrir l'effet.
Demain, c'est l'éclair dans la voile,
C'est le nuage sur l'étoile,
C'est un traître qui se dévoile,
C'est le bélier qui bat les tours,
C'est l'astre qui change de zone,
C'est Paris qui suit Babylone;
Demain, c'est le sapin du trône,
Aujourd'hui, c'en est le velours!

[II, 55–66]

Sur le bal de l'Hôtel de Ville

Ainsi l'Hôtel de Ville illumine son faîte.
Le prince et les flambeaux, tout y brille, et la fête
Ce soir va resplendir sur ce comble éclairé,
Comme l'idée au front du poète sacré!
Mais cette fête, amis, n'est pas une pensée.
Ce n'est pas d'un banquet que la France est pressée,
Et ce n'est pas un bal qu'il faut, en vérité,
A ce tas de douleurs qu'on nomme la cité!

Puissants! nous ferions mieux de panser quelque plaie
Dont le sage rêveur à cette heure s'effraie,
D'étayer l'escalier qui d'en bas monte en haut,
D'agrandir l'atelier, d'amoindrir l'échafaud,
De songer aux enfants qui sont sans pain dans l'ombre,
De rendre un paradis au pauvre impie et sombre,
Que d'allumer un lustre et de tenir la nuit
Quelques fous éveillés autour d'un peu de bruit!

O reines de nos toits, femmes chastes et saintes,
Fleurs qui de nos maisons parfumez les enceintes,
Vous à qui le bonheur conseille la vertu,
Vous qui contre le mal n'avez pas combattu,
A qui jamais la faim, empoisonneuse infâme,
N'a dit: Vends-moi ton corps, – c'est-à-dire votre âme!
Vous dont le cœur de joie et d'innocence est plein,
Dont la pudeur a plus d'enveloppes de lin
Que n'en avait Isis, la déesse voilée,
Cette fête est pour vous comme une aube étoilée!
Vous riez d'y courir tandis qu'on souffre ailleurs!
C'est que votre belle âme ignore les douleurs;
Le hasard vous posa dans la sphère suprême;
Vous vivez, vous brillez, vous ne voyez pas même,
Tant vos yeux éblouis de rayons sont noyés,
Ce qu'au-dessous de vous dans l'ombre on foule aux pieds!

Oui, c'est ainsi. – Le prince, et le riche, et le monde
Cherche à vous réjouir, vous pour qui tout abonde.
Vous avez la beauté, vous avez l'ornement;
La fête vous enivre à son bourdonnement,
Et, comme à la lumière un papillon de soie,
Vous volez à la porte ouverte qui flamboie!
Vous allez à ce bal, et vous ne songez pas
Que parmi ces passants amassés sur vos pas,
En foule émerveillés des chars et des livrées,
D'autres femmes sont là, non moins que vous parées,
Qu'on farde et qu'on expose à vendre au carrefour;
Spectres où saigne encor la place de l'amour;
Comme vous pour le bal, belles et demi-nues;
Pour vous voir au passage, hélas! exprès venues,
Voilant leur deuil affreux d'un sourire moqueur,
Les fleurs au front, la boue aux pieds, la haine au cœur!

Mai 1832

'L'aurore s'allume ...'

L'aurore s'allume,
L'ombre épaisse fuit;
Le rêve et la brume
Vont où va la nuit;
Paupières et roses
S'ouvrent demi-closes;
Du réveil des choses
On entend le bruit.

Tout chante et murmure,
Tout parle à la fois,
Fumée et verdure,
Les nids et les toits;
Le vent parle aux chênes,
L'eau parle aux fontaines;
Toutes les haleines
Deviennent des voix!

Tout reprend son âme,
L'enfant son hochet,
Le foyer sa flamme,
Le luth son archet;
Folie ou démence,
Dans le monde immense,
Chacun recommence
Ce qu'il ébauchait.

Qu'on pense ou qu'on aime,
Sans cesse agité,
Vers un but suprême,
Tout vole emporté;
L'esquif cherche un môle,
L'abeille un vieux saule,
La boussole un pôle,
Moi la vérité!

Décembre 1834

'Puisque j'ai mis ma lèvre...'

Puisque j'ai mis ma lèvre à ta coupe encor pleine;
Puisque j'ai dans tes mains posé mon front pâli;
Puisque j'ai respiré parfois la douce haleine
De ton âme, parfum dans l'ombre enseveli;

Puisqu'il me fut donné de t'entendre me dire
Les mots où se répand le cœur mystérieux;
Puisque j'ai vu pleurer, puisque j' ai vu sourire
Ta bouche sur ma bouche et tes yeux sur mes yeux;

Puisque j'ai vu briller sur ma tête ravie
Un rayon de ton astre, hélas! voilé toujours;
Puisque j'ai vu tomber dans l'onde de ma vie
Une feuille de rose arrachée à tes jours;

Je puis maintenant dire aux rapides années:
– Passez! passez toujours! je n'ai plus à vieillir!
Allez-vous-en avec vos fleurs toutes fanées;
J'ai dans l'âme une fleur que nul ne peut cueillir!

Votre aile en le heurtant ne fera rien répandre
Du vase où je m'abreuve et que j'ai bien rempli.
Mon âme a plus de feu que vous n'avez de cendre!
Mon cœur a plus d'amour que vous n'avez d'oubli!

1ᵉʳ janvier 1835. Minuit et demi

A Albert Dürer

Dans les vieilles forêts où la sève à grands flots
Court du fût noir de l'aulne au tronc blanc des bouleaux,
Bien des fois, n'est-ce pas ? à travers la clairière,
Pâle, effaré, n'osant regarder en arrière,
Tu t'es hâté, tremblant et d'un pas convulsif,
O mon maître Albert Düre, ô vieux peintre pensif !
On devine, devant tes tableaux qu'on vénère,
Que dans les noirs taillis ton œil visionnaire
Voyait distinctement, par l'ombre recouverts,
Le faune aux doigts palmés, le sylvain aux yeux verts,
Pan, qui revêt de fleurs l'antre où tu te recueilles,
Et l'antique dryade aux mains pleines de feuilles.

Une forêt pour toi, c'est un monde hideux.
Le songe et le réel s'y mêlent tous les deux.
Là se penchent rêveurs les vieux pins, les grands ormes
Dont les rameaux tordus font cent coudes difformes,
Et dans ce groupe sombre agité par le vent,
Rien n'est tout à fait mort ni tout à fait vivant.
Le cresson boit; l'eau court; les frênes sur les pentes,
Sous la broussaille horrible et les ronces grimpantes,
Contractent lentement leurs pieds noueux et noirs.
Les fleurs au cou de cygne ont les lacs pour miroirs;
Et sur vous qui passez et l'avez réveillée,
Mainte chimère étrange à la gorge écaillée,
D'un arbre entre ses doigts serrant les larges nœuds,
Du fond d'un antre obscur fixe un œil lumineux.
O végétation ! esprit ! matière ! force !
Couverte de peau rude ou de vivante écorce !

Aux bois, ainsi que toi, je n'ai jamais erré,
Maître, sans qu'en mon cœur l'horreur n'ait pénétré,
Sans voir tressaillir l'herbe, et, par le vent bercées,
Pendre à tous les rameaux de confuses pensées.
Dieu seul, ce grand témoin des faits mystérieux,
Dieu seul le sait, souvent, en de sauvages lieux,
J'ai senti, moi qu'échauffe une secrète flamme,
Comme moi palpiter et vivre avec une âme,
Et rire, et se parler dans l'ombre à demi-voix,
Les chênes monstrueux qui remplissent les bois.

20 avril 1837

'A quoi je songe? ...'

A quoi je songe? – Hélas! loin du toit où vous êtes,
Enfants, je songe à vous! à vous, mes jeunes têtes,
Espoir de mon été déjà penchant et mûr,
Rameaux dont, tous les ans, l'ombre croît sur mon mur!
Douces âmes à peine au jour épanouies,
Des rayons de votre aube encor tout éblouies!
Je songe aux deux petits qui pleurent en riant,
Et qui font gazouiller sur le seuil verdoyant,
Comme deux jeunes fleurs qui se heurtent entre elles,
Leurs jeux charmants mêlés de charmantes querelles!
Et puis, père inquiet, je rêve aux deux aînés
Qui s'avancent déjà de plus de flot baignés,
Laissant pencher parfois leur tête encor naïve,
L'un déjà curieux, l'autre déjà pensive!

Seul et triste au milieu des chants des matelots,
Le soir, sous la falaise, à cette heure où les flots,
S'ouvrant et se fermant comme autant de narines,
Mêlent au vent des cieux mille haleines marines,
Où l'on entend dans l'air d'ineffables échos
Qui viennent de la terre ou qui viennent des eaux,
Ainsi je songe! – à vous, enfants, maison, famille,
A la table qui rit, au foyer qui pétille,
A tous les soins pieux que répandent sur vous
Votre mère si tendre et votre aïeul si doux!
Et tandis qu'à mes pieds s'étend, couvert de voiles,
Le limpide océan, ce miroir des étoiles,
Tandis que les nochers laissent errer leurs yeux
De l'infini des mers à l'infini des cieux,
Moi, rêvant à vous seuls, je contemple et je sonde
L'amour que j'ai pour vous dans mon âme profonde,
Amour doux et puissant qui toujours m'est resté,
Et cette grande mer est petite à côté!

15 juillet 1837 – Fécamp
Ecrit au bord de la mer

Oceano nox

Saint-Valery-sur-Somme

Oh! combien de marins, combien de capitaines
Qui sont partis joyeux pour des courses lointaines,
Dans ce morne horizon se sont évanouis!
Combien ont disparu, dure et triste fortune!
Dans une mer sans fond, par une nuit sans lune,
Sous l'aveugle océan à jamais enfouis!

Combien de patrons morts avec leurs équipages!
L'ouragan de leur vie a pris toutes les pages,
Et d'un souffle il a tout dispersé sur les flots!
Nul ne saura leur fin dans l'abîme plongée.
Chaque vague en passant d'un butin s'est chargée;
L'une a saisi l'esquif, l'autre les matelots!

Nul ne sait votre sort, pauvres têtes perdues!
Vous roulez à travers les sombres étendues,
Heurtant de vos fronts morts des écueils inconnus.
Oh! que de vieux parents, qui n'avaient plus qu'un rêve,
Sont morts en attendant tous les jours sur la grève
                    Ceux qui ne sont pas revenus!

On s'entretient de vous parfois dans les veillées.
Maint joyeux cercle, assis sur des ancres rouillées,
Mêle encor quelque temps vos noms d'ombre couverts
Aux rires, aux refrains, aux récits d'aventures,
Aux baisers qu'on dérobe à vos belles futures,
Tandis que vous dormez dans les goémons verts!

On demande: – Où sont-ils? sont-ils rois dans quelque île?
Nous ont-ils délaissés pour un bord plus fertile? –
Puis votre souvenir même est enseveli.
Le corps se perd dans l'eau, le nom dans la mémoire.
Le temps, qui sur toute ombre en verse une plus noire,
Sur le sombre océan jette le sombre oubli.

Bientôt des yeux de tous votre ombre est disparue.
L'un n'a-t-il pas sa barque et l'autre sa charrue?
Seules, durant ces nuits où l'orage est vainqueur,
Vos veuves aux fronts blancs, lasses de vous attendre,
Parlent encor de vous en remuant la cendre
                    De leur foyer et de leur cœur!

Et quand la tombe enfin a fermé leur paupière,
Rien ne sait plus vos noms, pas même une humble pierre
Dans l'étroit cimetière où l'écho nous répond,
Pas même un saule vert qui s'effeuille à l'automne,
Pas même la chanson naïve et monotone
Que chante un mendiant à l'angle d'un vieux pont!

Où sont-ils, les marins sombrés dans les nuits noires?
O flots, que vous savez de lugubres histoires!
Flots profonds redoutés des mères à genoux!
Vous vous les racontez en montant les marées,
Et c'est ce qui vous fait ces voix désespérées
Que vous avez le soir quand vous venez vers nous!

Juillet 1836

Nuits de juin

L'été, lorsque le jour a fui, de fleurs couverte
La plaine verse au loin un parfum enivrant;
Les yeux fermés, l'oreille aux rumeurs entr'ouverte,
On ne dort qu'à demi d'un sommeil transparent.

Les astres sont plus purs, l'ombre paraît meilleure;
Un vague demi-jour teint le dôme éternel;
Et l'aube douce et pâle, en attendant son heure,
Semble toute la nuit errer au bas du ciel.

28 septembre 1837

Tristesse d'Olympio

Les champs n'étaient point noirs, les cieux n'étaient pas mornes.
Non, le jour rayonnait dans un azur sans bornes
      Sur la terre étendu,
L'air était plein d'encens et les prés de verdures
Quand il revit ces lieux où par tant de blessures
      Son cœur s'est répandu!

L'automne souriait; les coteaux vers la plaine
Penchaient leurs bois charmants qui jaunissaient à peine;
      Le ciel était doré;
Et les oiseaux, tournés vers celui que tout nomme,
Disant peut-être à Dieu quelque chose de l'homme,
      Chantaient leur chant sacré!

Il voulut tout revoir, l'étang près de la source,
La masure où l'aumône avait vidé leur bourse,
      Le vieux frêne plié,
Les retraites d'amour au fond des bois perdues,
L'arbre où dans les baisers leurs âmes confondues
      Avaient tout oublié!

Il chercha le jardin, la maison isolée,
La grille d'où l'œil plonge en une oblique allée,
      Les vergers en talus.
Pâle, il marchait. – Au bruit de son pas grave et sombre,
Il voyait à chaque arbre, hélas! se dresser l'ombre
      Des jours qui ne sont plus!

Il entendait frémir dans la forêt qu'il aime
Ce doux vent qui, faisant tout vibrer en nous-même,
      Y réveille l'amour,
Et, remuant le chêne ou balançant la rose,
Semble l'âme de tout qui va sur chaque chose
      Se poser tour à tour!

Les feuilles qui gisaient dans le bois solitaire,
S'efforçant sous ses pas de s'élever de terre,
      Couraient dans le jardin;
Ainsi, parfois, quand l'âme est triste, nos pensées
S'envolent un moment sur leurs ailes blessées,
      Puis retombent soudain.

Il contempla longtemps les formes magnifiques
Que la nature prend dans les champs pacifiques;
     Il rêva jusqu'au soir;
Tout le jour il erra le long de la ravine,
Admirant tour à tour le ciel, face divine,
     Le lac, divin miroir!

Hélas! se rappelant ses douces aventures,
Regardant, sans entrer, par-dessus les clôtures,
     Ainsi qu'un paria,
Il erra tout le jour. Vers l'heure où la nuit tombe,
Il se sentit le cœur triste comme une tombe;
     Alors il s'écria:

«O douleur! j'ai voulu, moi dont l'âme est troublée,
Savoir si l'urne encor conservait la liqueur,
Et voir ce qu'avait fait cette heureuse vallée
De tout ce que j'avais laissé là de mon cœur!

«Que peu de temps suffit pour changer toutes choses!
Nature au front serein, comme vous oubliez!
Et comme vous brisez dans vos métamorphoses
Les fils mystérieux où nos cœurs sont liés!

«Nos chambres de feuillage en halliers sont changées!
L'arbre où fut notre chiffre est mort ou renversé;
Nos roses dans l'enclos ont été ravagées
Par les petits enfants qui sautent le fossé.

«Un mur clôt la fontaine où, par l'heure échauffée,
Folâtre, elle buvait en descendant des bois;
Elle prenait de l'eau dans sa main, douce fée,
Et laissait retomber des perles de ses doigts!

«On a pavé la route âpre et mal aplanie,
Où, dans le sable pur se dessinant si bien,
Et de sa petitesse étalant l'ironie,
Son pied charmant semblait rire à côté du mien!

«La borne du chemin, qui vit des jours sans nombre,
Où jadis pour m'attendre elle aimait à s'asseoir,
S'est usée en heurtant, lorsque la route est sombre,
Les grands chars gémissants qui reviennent le soir.

«La forêt ici manque et là s'est agrandie.
De tout ce qui fut nous presque rien n'est vivant;
Et, comme un tas de cendre éteinte et refroidie,
L'amas des souvenirs se disperse à tout vent!

«N'existons-nous donc plus? Avons-nous eu notre heure?
Rien ne la rendra-t-il à nos cris superflus?
L'air joue avec la branche au moment où je pleure;
Ma maison me regarde et ne me connaît plus.

«D'autres vont maintenant passer où nous passâmes.
Nous y sommes venus, d'autres vont y venir;
Et le songe qu'avaient ébauché nos deux âmes,
Ils le continueront sans pouvoir le finir!

«Car personne ici-bas ne termine et n'achève;
Les pires des humains sont comme les meilleurs.
Nous nous réveillons tous au même endroit du rêve.
Tout commence en ce monde et tout finit ailleurs.

«Oui, d'autres à leur tour viendront, couples sans tache,
Puiser dans cet asile heureux, calme, enchanté,
Tout ce que la nature à l'amour qui se cache
Mêle de rêverie et de solennité!

«D'autres auront nos champs, nos sentiers, nos retraites;
Ton bois, ma bien-aimée, est à des inconnus.
D'autres femmes viendront, baigneuses indiscrètes,
Troubler le flot sacré qu'ont touché tes pieds nus!

«Quoi donc! c'est vainement qu'ici nous nous aimâmes!
Rien ne nous restera de ces coteaux fleuris
Où nous fondions notre être en y mêlant nos flammes!
L'impassible nature a déjà tout repris.

«Oh! dites-moi, ravins, frais ruisseaux, treilles mûres,
Rameaux chargés de nids, grottes, forêts, buissons,
Est-ce que vous ferez pour d'autres vos murmures?
Est-ce que vous direz à d'autres vos chansons? ·

«Nous vous comprenions tant! doux, attentifs, austères,
Tous nos échos s'ouvraient si bien à votre voix!
Et nous prêtions si bien, sans troubler vos mystères,
L'oreille aux mots profonds que vous dites parfois!

«Répondez, vallon pur, répondez, solitude,
O nature abritée en ce désert si beau,
Lorsque nous dormirons tous deux dans l'attitude
Que donne aux morts pensifs la forme du tombeau,

«Est-ce que vous serez à ce point insensible
De nous savoir couchés, morts avec nos amours,
Et de continuer votre fête paisible.
Et de toujours sourire et de chanter toujours?

«Est-ce que, nous sentant errer dans vos retraites,
Fantômes reconnus par vos monts et vos bois,
Vous ne nous direz pas de ces choses secrètes
Qu'on dit en revoyant des amis d'autrefois?

«Est-ce que vous pourrez, sans tristesse et sans plainte,
Voir nos ombres flotter où marchèrent nos pas,
Et la voir m'entraîner, dans une morne étreinte,
Vers quelque source en pleurs qui sanglote tout bas?

«Et s'il est quelque part, dans l'ombre où rien ne veille,
Deux amants sous vos fleurs abritant leurs transports,
Ne leur irez-vous pas murmurer à l'oreille:
– Vous qui vivez, donnez une pensée aux morts!

«Dieu nous prête un moment les prés et les fontaines,
Les grands bois frissonnants, les rocs profonds et sourds,
Et les cieux azurés et les lacs et les plaines,
Pour y mettre nos cœurs, nos rêves, nos amours;

«Puis il nous les retire. Il souffle notre flamme;
Il plonge dans la nuit l'antre où nous rayonnons;
Et dit à la vallée, où s'imprima notre âme,
D'effacer notre trace et d'oublier nos noms.

«Eh bien! oubliez-nous, maison, jardin, ombrages!
Herbe, use notre seuil! ronce, cache nos pas!
Chantez, oiseaux! ruisseaux, coulez! croissez, feuillages!
Ceux que vous oubliez ne vous oublieront pas.

«Car vous êtes pour nous l'ombre de l'amour même!
Vous êtes l'oasis qu'on rencontre en chemin!
Vous êtes, ô vallon, la retraite suprême
Où nous avons pleuré nous tenant par la main!

«Toutes les passions s'éloignent avec l'âge,
L'une emportant son masque et l'autre son couteau,
Comme un essaim chantant d'histrions en voyage
Dont le groupe décroît derrière le coteau.

«Mais toi, rien ne t'efface, amour! toi qui nous charmes,
Toi qui, torche ou flambeau, luis dans notre brouillard!
Tu nous tiens par la joie, et surtout par les larmes.
Jeune homme on te maudit, on t'adore vieillard.

«Dans ces jours où la tête au poids des ans s'incline,
Où l'homme, sans projets, sans but, sans visions,
Sent qu'il n'est déjà plus qu'une tombe en ruine
Où gisent ses vertus et ses illusions;

«Quand notre âme en rêvant descend dans nos entrailles,
Comptant dans notre cœur, qu'enfin la glace atteint,
Comme on compte les morts sur un champ de batailles,
Chaque douleur tombée et chaque songe éteint,

«Comme quelqu'un qui cherche en tenant une lampe,
Loin des objets réels, loin du monde rieur,
Elle arrive à pas lents par une obscure rampe
Jusqu'au fond désolé du gouffre intérieur;

«Et là, dans cette nuit qu'aucun rayon n'étoile,
L'âme, en un repli sombre où tout semble finir,
Sent quelque chose encor palpiter sous un voile ... –
C'est toi qui dors dans l'ombre, ô sacré souvenir!»

21 octobre 1837

[*p.* 62]

Le chant de ceux qui s'en vont sur mer

AIR BRETON

> Adieu, patrie!
> L'onde est en furie.
> Adieu, patrie!
> Azur!

Adieu, maison, treille au fruit mûr,
Adieu, les fleurs d'or du vieux mur!

> Adieu, patrie!
> Ciel, forêt, prairie!
> Adieu, patrie,
> Azur!

> Adieu, patrie!
> L'onde est en furie.
> Adieu, patrie,
> Azur!

Adieu, fiancée au front pur,
Le ciel est noir, le vent est dur.

> Adieu, patrie!
> Lise, Anna, Marie!
> Adieu, patrie,
> Azur!

> Adieu, patrie!
> L'onde est en furie.
> Adieu, patrie,
> Azur!

Notre œil, que voile un deuil futur,
Va du flot sombre au sort obscur!

> Adieu, patrie!
> Pour toi mon cœur prie.
> Adieu, patrie,
> Azur!

En mer. 1er août 1852

Le chasseur noir

Qu'es-tu, passant? Le bois est sombre,
Les corbeaux volent en grand nombre,
    Il va pleuvoir.
– Je suis celui qui va dans l'ombre,
    Le Chasseur Noir!

Les feuilles des bois, du vent remuées,
    Sifflent... on dirait
Qu'un sabbat nocturne emplit de huées
    Toute la forêt;
Dans une clairière au sein des nuées
    La lune apparaît.

    – Chasse le daim, chasse la biche,
Cours dans les bois, cours dans la friche,
    Voici le soir.
Chasse le czar, chasse l'Autriche,
    O Chasseur Noir!

Les feuilles des bois –

    Souffle en ton cor, boucle ta guêtre,
Chasse les cerfs qui viennent paître
    Près du manoir.
Chasse le roi, chasse le prêtre,
    O Chasseur Noir!

Les feuilles des bois –

    Il tonne, il pleut, c'est le déluge.
Le renard fuit, pas de refuge
    Et pas d'espoir!
Chasse l'espion, chasse le juge,
    O Chasseur Noir!

Les feuilles des bois –

    Tous les démons de saint-Antoine
Bondissent dans la folle avoine
    Sans t'émouvoir;
Chasse l'abbé, chasse le moine,
    O Chasseur Noir!

Les feuilles des bois –

    Chasse les ours! ta meute jappe.
    Que pas un sanglier n'échappe!
        Fais ton devoir!
    Chasse César, chasse le pape,
        O Chasseur Noir!

Les feuilles des bois –

    Le loup de ton sentier s'écarte.
    Que ta meute à sa suite parte!
        Cours! fais-le choir!
    Chasse le brigand Bonaparte,
        O Chasseur Noir!

Les feuilles des bois, du vent remuées,
    Tombent . . . on dirait
Que le sabbat sombre aux rauques huées
    A fui la forêt;
Le clair chant du coq perce les nuées;
    Ciel! l'aube apparaît!

    Tout reprend sa forme première.
    Tu redeviens la France altière
        Si belle à voir,
    L'ange blanc vêtu de lumière,
        O Chasseur Noir!

Les feuilles des bois, du vent remuées,
    Tombent . . . on dirait
Que le sabbat sombre aux rauques huées
    A fui la forêt;
Le clair chant du coq perce les nuées,
    Ciel! l'aube apparaît!

Jersey. 22 Octobre 1852

L'expiation, 1

Il neigeait. On était vaincu par sa conquête.
Pour la première fois l'aigle baissait la tête.
Sombres jours! l'empereur revenait lentement,
Laissant derrière lui brûler Moscou fumant.
Il neigeait. L'âpre hiver fondait en avalanche.
Après la plaine blanche une autre plaine blanche.
On ne connaissait plus les chefs ni le drapeau.
Hier la grande armée, et maintenant troupeau.
On ne distinguait plus les ailes ni le centre.
Il neigeait. Les blessés s'abritaient dans le ventre
Des chevaux morts; au seuil des bivouacs désolés
On voyait des clairons à leur poste gelés,
Restés debout, en selle et muets, blancs de givre,
Collant leur bouche en pierre aux trompettes de cuivre.
Boulets, mitraille, obus, mêlés aux flocons blancs,
Pleuvaient; les grenadiers, surpris d'être tremblants,
Marchaient pensifs, la glace à leur moustache grise.
Il neigeait, il neigeait toujours! La froide bise
Sifflait; sur le verglas, dans des lieux inconnus,
On n'avait pas de pain et l'on allait pieds nus.
Ce n'étaient plus des cœurs vivants, des gens de guerre:
C'était un rêve errant dans la brume, un mystère,
Une procession d'ombres sous le ciel noir.
La solitude vaste, épouvantable à voir,
Partout apparaissait, muette vengeresse.
Le ciel faisait sans bruit avec la neige épaisse
Pour cette immense armée un immense linceul.
Et chacun se sentant mourir, on était seul.
– Sortira-t-on jamais de ce funeste empire?
Deux ennemis! le czar, le nord. Le nord est pire.
On jetait les canons pour brûler les affûts.
Qui se couchait, mourait. Groupe morne et confus,
Ils fuyaient; le désert dévorait le cortège.
On pouvait, à des plis qui soulevaient la neige,
Voir que des régiments s'étaient endormis là.
O chutes d'Annibal! lendemains d'Attila!
Fuyards, blessés, mourants, caissons, brancards, civières,
On s'écrasait aux ponts pour passer les rivières,
On s'endormait dix mille, on se réveillait cent.
Ney, que suivait naguère une armée, à présent
S'évadait, disputant sa montre à trois cosaques.
Toutes les nuits, qui vive! alerte, assauts! attaques!
Ces fantômes prenaient leur fusil, et sur eux
Ils voyaient se ruer, effrayants, ténébreux,
Avec des cris pareils aux voix des vautours chauves,

D'horribles escadrons, tourbillons d'hommes fauves.
Toute une armée ainsi dans la nuit se perdait.
L'empereur était là, debout, qui regardait.
Il était comme un arbre en proie à la cognée.
Sur ce géant, grandeur jusqu'alors épargnée,
Le malheur, bûcheron sinistre, était monté;
Et lui, chêne vivant, par la hache insulté,
Tressaillant sous le spectre aux lugubres revanches,
Il regardait tomber autour de lui ses branches.
Chefs, soldats, tous mouraient. Chacun avait son tour.
Tandis qu'environnant sa tente avec amour,
Voyant son ombre aller et venir sur la toile,
Ceux qui restaient, croyant toujours à son étoile,
Accusaient le destin de lèse-majesté,
Lui se sentit soudain dans l'âme épouvanté.
Stupéfait du désastre et ne sachant que croire,
L'empereur se tourna vers Dieu; l'homme de gloire
Trembla; Napoléon comprit qu'il expiait
Quelque chose peut-être, et, livide, inquiet,
Devant ses légions sur la neige semées:
«Est-ce le châtiment, dit-il, Dieu des armées?»
Alors il s'entendit appeler par son nom
Et quelqu'un qui parlait dans l'ombre lui dit: Non.

Souvenir de la nuit du 4

L'enfant avait reçu deux balles dans la tête.
Le logis était propre, humble, paisible, honnête;
On voyait un rameau bénit sur un portrait.
Une vieille grand'mère était là qui pleurait.
Nous le déshabillions en silence. Sa bouche,
Pâle, s'ouvrait; la mort noyait son œil farouche;
Ses bras pendants semblaient demander des appuis.
Il avait dans sa poche une toupie en buis.
On pouvait mettre un doigt dans les trous de ses plaies.
Avez-vous vu saigner la mûre dans les haies?
Son crâne était ouvert comme un bois qui se fend.
L'aïeule regarda déshabiller l'enfant,
Disant: — Comme il est blanc! approchez donc la lampe.
Dieu! ses pauvres cheveux sont collés sur sa tempe! —
Et quand ce fut fini, le prit sur ses genoux.
La nuit était lugubre; on entendait des coups

De fusil dans la rue où l'on en tuait d'autres.
– Il faut ensevelir l'enfant, dirent les nôtres.
Et l'on prit un drap blanc dans l'armoire en noyer.
L'aïeule cependant l'approchait du foyer
Comme pour réchauffer ses membres déjà roides.
Hélas! ce que la mort touche de ses mains froides
Ne se réchauffe plus aux foyers d'ici-bas!
Elle pencha la tête et lui tira ses bas,
Et dans ses vieilles mains prit les pieds du cadavre.
– Est-ce que ce n'est pas une chose qui navre!
Cria-t-elle; monsieur, il n'avait pas huit ans!
Ses maîtres, il allait en classe, étaient contents.
Monsieur, quand il fallait que je fisse une lettre,
C'est lui qui l'écrivait. Est-ce qu'on va se mettre
A tuer les enfants maintenant? Ah! mon Dieu!
On est donc des brigands! Je vous demande un peu,
Il jouait ce matin, là, devant la fenêtre!
Dire qu'ils m'ont tué ce pauvre petit être!
Il passait dans la rue, ils ont tiré dessus.
Monsieur, il était bon et doux comme un Jésus.
Moi je suis vieille, il est tout simple que je parte;
Cela n'aurait rien fait à monsieur Bonaparte
De me tuer au lieu de tuer mon enfant! –
Elle s'interrompit, les sanglots l'étouffant,
Puis elle dit, et tous pleuraient près de l'aïeule:
– Que vais-je devenir à présent toute seule?
Expliquez-moi cela, vous autres, aujourd'hui.
Hélas! je n'avais plus de sa mère que lui.
Pourquoi l'a-t-on tué? je veux qu'on me l'explique.
L'enfant n'a pas crié vive la République. –

Nous nous taisions, debout et graves, chapeau bas,
Tremblant devant ce deuil qu'on ne console pas.

Vous ne compreniez point, mère, la politique.
Monsieur Napoléon, c'est son nom authentique,
Est pauvre, et même prince; il aime les palais;
Il lui convient d'avoir des chevaux, des valets,
De l'argent pour son jeu, sa table, son alcôve,
Ses chasses; par la même occasion, il sauve
La famille, l'église et la société;
Il veut avoir Saint-Cloud, plein de roses l'été,
Où viendront l'adorer les préfets et les maires;
C'est pour cela qu'il faut que les vieilles grand'mères,
De leurs pauvres doigts gris que fait trembler le temps,
Cousent dans le linceul des enfants de sept ans.

 [pp. 70–72]

'Sonnez, sonnez toujours . . .'

Sonnez, sonnez toujours, clairons de la pensée.

Quand Josué rêveur, la tête aux cieux dressée,
Suivi des siens, marchait, et, prophète irrité,
Sonnait de la trompette autour de la cité,
Au premier tour qu'il fit, le roi se mit à rire;
Au second tour, riant toujours, il lui fit dire:
«Crois-tu donc renverser ma ville avec du vent?»
A la troisième fois l'arche allait en avant,
Puis les trompettes, puis toute l'armée en marche,
Et les petits enfants venaient cracher sur l'arche,
Et, soufflant dans leur trompe, imitaient le clairon;
Au quatrième tour, bravant les fils d'Aaron,
Entre les vieux créneaux tout brunis par la rouille,
Les femmes s'asseyaient en filant leur quenouille,
Et se moquaient, jetant des pierres aux hébreux;
A la cinquième fois, sur ces murs ténébreux,
Aveugles et boiteux vinrent, et leurs huées
Raillaient le noir clairon sonnant sous les nuées;
A la sixième fois, sur sa tour de granit
Si haute qu'au sommet l'aigle faisait son nid,
Si dure que l'éclair l'eût en vain foudroyée,
Le roi revint, riant à gorge déployée,
Et cria: «Ces hébreux sont bons musiciens!»
Autour du roi joyeux riaient tous les anciens
Qui le soir sont assis au temple, et délibèrent.

A la septième fois, les murailles tombèrent.

Mes deux filles

Dans le frais clair-obscur du soir charmant qui tombe,
L'une pareille au cygne et l'autre à la colombe,
Belles, et toutes deux joyeuses, ô douceur!
Voyez, la grande sœur et la petite sœur
Sont assises au seuil du jardin, et sur elles
Un bouquet d'œillets blancs aux longues tiges frêles,

Dans une urne de marbre agité par le vent,
Se penche, et les regarde, immobile et vivant,
Et frissonne dans l'ombre, et semble, au bord du vase,
Un vol de papillons arrêté dans l'extase.

La Terrasse, près Enghien, juin 1842

Vieille chanson du jeune temps

Je ne songeais pas à Rose;
Rose au bois vint avec moi;
Nous parlions de quelque chose,
Mais je ne sais plus de quoi.

J'étais froid comme les marbres;
Je marchais à pas distraits;
Je parlais des fleurs, des arbres;
Son œil semblait dire: «Après?»

La rosée offrait ses perles,
Le taillis ses parasols;
J'allais; j'écoutais les merles,
Et Rose les rossignols.

Moi, seize ans, et l'air morose.
Elle vingt; ses yeux brillaient.
Les rossignols chantaient Rose,
Et les merles me sifflaient.

Rose, droite sur ses hanches,
Leva son beau bras tremblant
Pour prendre une mûre aux branches;
Je ne vis pas son bras blanc.

Une eau courait, fraîche et creuse,
Sur les mousses de velours;
Et la nature amoureuse
Dormait dans les grands bois sourds.

[*pp.* 74–75]

Rose défit sa chaussure,
Et mit, d'un air ingénu,
Son petit pied dans l'eau pure;
Je ne vis pas son pied nu.

Je ne savais que lui dire;
Je la suivais dans le bois,
La voyant parfois sourire
Et soupirer quelquefois.

Je ne vis qu'elle était belle
Qu'en sortant des grands bois sourds.
– Soit; n'y pensons plus! dit-elle.
Depuis, j'y pense toujours.

Paris, juin 1831

L'enfance

L'enfant chantait; la mère au lit, exténuée,
Agonisait, beau front dans l'ombre se penchant;
La mort au-dessus d'elle errait dans la nuée;
Et j'écoutais ce râle, et j'entendais ce chant.

L'enfant avait cinq ans, et près de la fenêtre,
Ses rires et ses jeux faisaient un charmant bruit;
Et la mère, à côté de ce pauvre doux être
Qui chantait tout le jour, toussait toute la nuit.

La mère alla dormir sous les dalles du cloître;
Et le petit enfant se remit à chanter . . . –
La douleur est un fruit; Dieu ne le fait pas croître
Sur la branche trop faible encor pour le porter.

Paris, janvier 1835

Unité

Par-dessus l'horizon aux collines brunies,
Le soleil, cette fleur des splendeurs infinies,
Se penchait sur la terre à l'heure du couchant;
Une humble marguerite, éclose au bord d'un champ,
Sur un mur gris, croulant parmi l'avoine folle,
Blanche, épanouissait sa candide auréole;
Et la petite fleur, par-dessus le vieux mur,
Regardait fixement, dans l'éternel azur,
Le grand astre épanchant sa lumière immortelle.
– Et moi, j'ai des rayons aussi! lui disait-elle.

Granville, juillet 1836

Premier mai

Tout conjugue le verbe aimer. Voici les roses.
Je ne suis pas en train de parler d'autres choses.
Premier mai! L'amour gai, triste, brûlant, jaloux,
Fait soupirer les bois, les nids, les fleurs, les loups;
L'arbre où j'ai, l'autre automne, écrit une devise,
La redit pour son compte et croit qu'il l'improvise;
Les vieux antres pensifs, dont rit le geai moqueur,
Clignent leurs gros sourcils et font la bouche en cœur;
L'atmosphère, embaumée et tendre, semble pleine
Des déclarations qu'au Printemps fait la plaine,
Et que l'herbe amoureuse adresse au ciel charmant.
A chaque pas du jour dans le bleu firmament,
La campagne éperdue, et toujours plus éprise,
Prodigue les senteurs, et, dans la tiède brise,
Envoie au renouveau ses baisers odorants;
Tous ses bouquets, azurs, carmins, pourpres, safrans,
Dont l'haleine s'envole en murmurant: Je t'aime!
Sur le ravin, l'étang, le pré, le sillon même,
Font des taches partout de toutes les couleurs;
Et, donnant les parfums, elle a gardé les fleurs;
Comme si ses soupirs et ses tendres missives
Au mois de mai, qui rit dans les branches lascives,
Et tous les billets doux de son amour bavard,
Avaient laissé leur trace aux pages du buvard!

[pp. 78–79]

Les oiseaux dans les bois, molles voix étouffées,
Chantent des triolets et des rondeaux aux fées;
Tout semble confier à l'ombre un doux secret;
Tout aime, et tout l'avoue à voix basse; on dirait
Qu'au nord, au sud brûlant, au couchant, à l'aurore,
La haie en fleur, le lierre et la source sonore,
Les monts, les champs, les lacs et les chênes mouvants
Répètent un quatrain fait par les quatre vents.

Saint-Germain, mai 18 . . .

Le rouet d'Omphale

Il est dans l'atrium, le beau rouet d'ivoire.
La roue agile est blanche, et la quenouille est noire;
La quenouille est d'ébène incrusté de lapis.
Il est dans l'atrium sur un riche tapis.

Un ouvrier d'Egine a sculpté sur la plinthe
Europe, dont un dieu n'écoute pas la plainte.
Le taureau blanc l'emporte. Europe, sans espoir,
Crie, et, baissant les yeux, s'épouvante de voir
L'Océan monstrueux qui baise ses pieds roses.

Des aiguilles, du fil, des boîtes demi-closes,
Les laines de Milet, peintes de pourpre et d'or,
Emplissent un panier près du rouet qui dort.

Cependant, odieux, effroyables, énormes,
Dans le fond du palais, vingt fantômes difformes,
Vingt monstres tout sanglants, qu'on ne voit qu'à demi,
Errent en foule autour du rouet endormi:
Le lion néméen, l'hydre affreuse de Lerne,
Cacus, le noir brigand de la noire caverne,
Le triple Géryon, et les typhons des eaux
Qui le soir à grand bruit soufflent dans les roseaux;
De la massue au front tous ont l'empreinte horrible,
Et tous, sans approcher, rôdant d'un air terrible,
Sur le rouet, où pend un fil souple et lié,
Fixent de loin dans l'ombre un œil humilié.

Juin 18 . . .

Lettre

Tu vois cela d'ici. – Des ocres et des craies,
Plaines où les sillons croisent leurs mille raies,
Chaumes à fleur de terre et que masque un buisson,
Quelques meules de foin debout sur le gazon,
De vieux toits enfumant le paysage bistre,
Un fleuve qui n'est pas le Gange ou le Caystre,
Pauvre cours d'eau normand troublé de sels marins,
A droite, vers le nord, de bizarres terrains
Pleins d'angles qu'on dirait façonnés à la pelle,
Voilà les premiers plans; une ancienne chapelle
Y mêle son aiguille, et range à ses côtés
Quelques ormes tortus, aux profils irrités,
Qui semblent, fatigués du zéphyr qui s'en joue,
Faire une remontrance au vent qui les secoue.
Une grosse charrette au coin de ma maison
Se rouille, et devant moi j'ai le vaste horizon
Dont la mer bleue emplit toutes les échancrures.
Des poules et des coqs, étalant leurs dorures,
Causent sous ma fenêtre, et les greniers des toits
Me jettent, par instants, des chansons en patois.
Dans mon allée habite un cordier patriarche,
Vieux qui fait bruyamment tourner sa roue, et marche
A reculons, son chanvre autour des reins tordu.
J'aime ces flots où court le grand vent éperdu;
Les champs à promener tout le jour me convient;
Les petits villageois, leur livre en main, m'envient,
Chez le maître d'école où je me suis logé,
Comme un grand écolier abusant d'un congé.
Le ciel rit, l'air est pur; tout le jour, chez mon hôte,
C'est un doux bruit d'enfants épelant à voix haute;
L'eau coule, un verdier passe; et, moi, je dis: Merci!
Merci, Dieu tout-puissant! – Ainsi je vis; ainsi,
Paisible, heure par heure, à petit bruit j'épanche
Mes jours, tout en songeant à vous, ma beauté blanche!
J'écoute les enfants jaser, et, par moment
Je vois en pleine mer passer superbement,
Au-dessus des pignons du tranquille village,
Quelque navire ailé qui fait un long voyage,
Et fuit sur l'océan, par tous les vents traqué,
Qui naguère dormait au port, le long du quai,
Et que n'ont retenu, loin des vagues jalouses,
Ni les pleurs des parents, ni l'effroi des épouses,
Ni le sombre reflet des écueils dans les eaux,
Ni l'importunité des sinistres oiseaux.

   Près Le Tréport, juin 18 . . .

'Viens! – une flûte invisible . . .'

Viens! – une flûte invisible
Soupire dans les vergers. –
La chanson la plus paisible
Est la chanson des bergers.

Le vent ride, sous l'yeuse,
Le sombre miroir des eaux. –
La chanson la plus joyeuse
Est la chanson des oiseaux.

Que nul soin ne te tourmente.
Aimons-nous! aimons toujours! –
La chanson la plus charmante
Est la chanson des amours.

    Les Metz, août 18 . . .

Paroles dans l'ombre

Elle disait: C'est vrai, j'ai tort de vouloir mieux;
Les heures sont ainsi très doucement passées;
Vous êtes là; mes yeux ne quittent pas vos yeux
Où je regarde aller et venir vos pensées.

Vous voir est un bonheur; je ne l'ai pas complet.
Sans doute, c'est encor bien charmant de la sorte!
Je veille, car je sais tout ce qui vous déplaît,
A ce que nul fâcheux ne vienne ouvrir la porte;

Je me fais bien petite en mon coin près de vous;
Vous êtes mon lion, je suis votre colombe;
J'entends de vos papiers le bruit paisible et doux;
Je ramasse parfois votre plume qui tombe;

Sans doute, je vous ai; sans doute, je vous voi.
La pensée est un vin dont les rêveurs sont ivres,
Je le sais; mais, pourtant, je veux qu'on songe à moi.
Quand vous êtes ainsi tout un soir dans vos livres,

Sans relever la tête et sans me dire un mot,
Une ombre reste au fond de mon cœur qui vous aime;
Et, pour que je vous voie entièrement, il faut
Me regarder un peu, de temps en temps, vous-même.

Paris, novembre 18 . . .

Un soir que je regardais le ciel

Elle me dit, un soir, en souriant:
– Ami, pourquoi contemplez-vous sans cesse
Le jour qui fuit, ou l'ombre qui s'abaisse,
Ou l'astre d'or qui monte à l'orient?
Que font vos yeux là-haut? je les réclame.
Quittez le ciel; regardez dans mon âme!

Dans ce ciel vaste, ombre où vous vous plaisez,
Où vos regards démesurés vont lire,
Qu'apprendrez-vous qui vaille mon sourire?
Qu'apprendras-tu qui vaille nos baisers?
Oh! de mon cœur lève les chastes voiles.
Si tu savais comme il est plein d'étoiles!

Que de soleils! Vois-tu, quand nous aimons,
Tout est en nous un radieux spectacle.
Le dévouement, rayonnant sur l'obstacle,
Vaut bien Vénus qui brille sur les monts.
Le vaste azur n'est rien, je te l'atteste;
Le ciel que j'ai dans l'âme est plus céleste!

C'est beau de voir un astre s'allumer.
Le monde est plein de merveilleuses choses.
Douce est l'aurore et douces sont les roses.
Rien n'est si doux que le charme d'aimer!
La clarté vraie et la meilleure flamme,
C'est le rayon qui va de l'âme à l'âme!

L'amour vaut mieux, au fond des antres frais,
Que ces soleils qu'on ignore et qu'on nomme.
Dieu mit, sachant ce qui convient à l'homme,
Le ciel bien loin et la femme tout près.
Il dit à ceux qui scrutent l'azur sombre:
«Vivez! aimez! le reste, c'est mon ombre!»

[pp. 85–86]

Aimons! c'est tout. Et Dieu le veut ainsi.
Laisse ton ciel que de froids rayons dorent!
Tu trouveras dans deux yeux qui t'adorent
Plus de beauté, plus de lumière aussi!
Aimer, c'est voir, sentir, rêver, comprendre.
L'esprit plus grand s'ajoute au cœur plus tendre.

Viens, bien-aimé! n'entends-tu pas toujours
Dans nos transports une harmonie étrange?
Autour de nous la nature se change
En une lyre et chante nos amours.
Viens! aimons-nous! errons sur la pelouse.
Ne songe plus au ciel! j'en suis jalouse! –

Ma bien-aimée ainsi tout bas parlait,
Avec son front posé sur sa main blanche,
Et l'œil rêveur d'un ange qui se penche,
Et sa voix grave, et cet air qui me plaît;
Belle et tranquille, et de me voir charmée,
Ainsi tout bas parlait ma bien-aimée.

Nos cœurs battaient; l'extase m'étouffait;
Les fleurs du soir entr'ouvraient leurs corolles . . .
Qu'avez-vous fait, arbres, de nos paroles?
De nos soupirs, rochers, qu'avez-vous fait?
C'est un destin bien triste que le nôtre,
Puisqu'un tel jour s'envole comme un autre!

O souvenirs! trésor dans l'ombre accru!
Sombre horizon des anciennes pensées!
Chère lueur des choses éclipsées!
Rayonnement du passé disparu!
Comme du seuil et du dehors d'un temple,
L'œil de l'esprit en rêvant vous contemple!

Quand les beaux jours font place aux jours amers,
De tout bonheur il faut quitter l'idée;
Quand l'espérance est tout à fait vidée,
Laissons tomber la coupe au fond des mers.
L'oubli! l'oubli! c'est l'onde où tout se noie;
C'est la mer sombre où l'on jette sa joie.

Montf., septembre 18 . . . – Brux., janvier 18 . . .

Écrit au bas d'un crucifix

Vous qui pleurez, venez à ce Dieu, car il pleure.
Vous qui souffrez, venez à lui, car il guérit.
Vous qui tremblez, venez à lui, car il sourit.
Vous qui passez, venez à lui, car il demeure.

Mars 1842

Écrit sur la plinthe d'un bas-relief antique

à Mademoiselle Louise B.

La musique est dans tout. Un hymne sort du monde.
Rumeur de la galère aux flancs lavés par l'onde,
Bruits des villes, pitié de la sœur pour la sœur,
Passion des amants jeunes et beaux, douceur
Des vieux époux usés ensemble par la vie,
Fanfare de la plaine émaillée et ravie,
Mots échangés le soir sur les seuils fraternels,
Sombre tressaillement des chênes éternels,
Vous êtes l'harmonie et la musique même!
Vous êtes les soupirs qui font le chant suprême!
Pour notre âme, les jours, la vie et les saisons,
Les songes de nos cœurs, les plis des horizons,
L'aube et ses pleurs, le soir et ses grands incendies,
Flottent dans un réseau de vagues mélodies.
Une voix dans les champs nous parle, une autre voix
Dit à l'homme autre chose et chante dans les bois.
Par moment, un troupeau bêle, une cloche tinte.
Quand par l'ombre, la nuit, la colline est atteinte,
De toutes parts on voit danser et resplendir,
Dans le ciel étoilé du zénith au nadir,
Dans la voix des oiseaux, dans le cri des cigales,
Le groupe éblouissant des notes inégales.
Toujours avec notre âme un doux bruit s'accoupla;
La nature nous dit: Chante! Et c'est pour cela
Qu'un statuaire ancien sculpta sur cette pierre
Un pâtre sur sa flûte abaissant sa paupière.

Juin 1833

'La clarté du dehors...'

La clarté du dehors ne distrait pas mon âme.
La plaine chante et rit comme une jeune femme;
      Le nid palpite dans les houx;
Partout la gaîté luit dans les bouches ouvertes;
Mai, couché dans la mousse au fond des grottes vertes,
      Fait aux amoureux les yeux doux.

Dans les champs de luzerne et dans les champs de fèves,
Les vagues papillons errent, pareils aux rêves;
      Le blé vert sort des sillons bruns;
Et les abeilles d'or courent à la pervenche,
Au thym, au liseron, qui tend son urne blanche
      A ces buveuses de parfums.

La nue étale au ciel ses pourpres et ses cuivres;
Les arbres, tout gonflés de printemps, semblent ivres;
      Les branches, dans leurs doux ébats,
Se jettent les oiseaux du bout de leurs raquettes;
Le bourdon galonné fait aux roses coquettes
      Des propositions tout bas.

Moi, je laisse voler les senteurs et les baumes,
Je laisse chuchoter les fleurs, ces doux fantômes,
      Et l'aube dire: Vous vivrez!
Je regarde en moi-même, et, seul, oubliant l'heure,
L'œil plein des visions de l'ombre intérieure,
      Je songe aux morts, ces délivrés.

Encore un peu de temps, encore, ô mer superbe,
Quelques reflux; j'aurai ma tombe aussi dans l'herbe,
      Blanche au milieu du frais gazon,
A l'ombre de quelque arbre où le lierre s'attache;
On y lira: – Passant, cette pierre te cache
      La ruine d'une prison.

Ingouville, mai 1843

'L'enfant, voyant l'aïeule . . .'

L'enfant, voyant l'aïeule à filer occupée,
Veut faire une quenouille à sa grande poupée.
L'aïeule s'assoupit un peu; c'est le moment.
L'enfant vient par derrière, et tire doucement
Un brin de la quenouille où le fuseau tournoie,
Puis s'enfuit triomphante, emportant avec joie
La belle laine d'or que le safran jaunit,
Autant qu'en pourrait prendre un oiseau pour son nid.

Cauterets, 25 août 1843

'J'aime l'araignée . . .'

J'aime l'araignée et j'aime l'ortie,
    Parce qu'on les hait;
Et que rien n'exauce et que tout châtie
    Leur morne souhait;

Parce qu'elles sont maudites, chétives,
    Noirs êtres rampants;
Parce qu'elles sont les tristes captives
    De leur guet-apens;

Parce qu'elles sont prises dans leur œuvre;
    O sort! fatals nœuds!
Parce que l'ortie est une couleuvre,
    L'araignée un gueux;

Parce qu'elles ont l'ombre des abîmes,
    Parce qu'on les fuit,
Parce qu'elles sont toutes deux victimes
    De la sombre nuit.

Passants, faites grâce à la plante obscure,
    Au pauvre animal.
Plaignez la laideur, plaignez la piqûre,
    Oh! plaignez le mal!

[pp. 92–93]

Il n'est rien qui n'ait sa mélancolie;
    Tout veut un baiser.
Dans leur fauve horreur, pour peu qu'on oublie
    De les écraser,

Pour peu qu'on leur jette un œil moins superbe,
    Tout bas, loin du jour,
La vilaine bête et la mauvaise herbe
    Murmurent: Amour!

Juillet 1842

'Elle avait pris ce pli . . .'

Elle avait pris ce pli dans son âge enfantin
De venir dans ma chambre un peu chaque matin;
Je l'attendais ainsi qu'un rayon qu'on espère;
Elle entrait, et disait: Bonjour, mon petit père;
Prenait ma plume, ouvrait mes livres, s'asseyait
Sur mon lit, dérangeait mes papiers, et riait,
Puis soudain s'en allait comme un oiseau qui passe.
Alors, je reprenais, la tête un peu moins lasse,
Mon œuvre interrompue, et, tout en écrivant,
Parmi mes manuscrits je rencontrais souvent
Quelque arabesque folle et qu'elle avait tracée,
Et mainte page blanche entre ses mains froissée
Où, je ne sais comment, venaient mes plus doux vers.
Elle aimait Dieu, les fleurs, les astres, les prés verts,
Et c'était un esprit avant d'être une femme.
Son regard reflétait la clarté de son âme.
Elle me consultait sur tout à tous moments.
Oh! que de soirs d'hiver radieux et charmants
Passés à raisonner langue, histoire et grammaire,
Mes quatre enfants groupés sur mes genoux, leur mère
Tout près, quelques amis causant au coin du feu!
J'appelais cette vie être content de peu!
Et dire qu'elle est morte! Hélas! que Dieu m'assiste!
Je n'étais jamais gai quand je la sentais triste;
J'étais morne au milieu du bal le plus joyeux
Si j'avais, en partant, vu quelque ombre en ses yeux.

Novembre 1846, jour des Morts

'Quand nous habitions tous ensemble ...'

Quand nous habitions tous ensemble
Sur nos collines d'autrefois,
Où l'eau court, où le buisson tremble,
Dans la maison qui touche au bois,

Elle avait dix ans, et moi trente;
J'étais pour elle l'univers.
Oh! comme l'herbe est odorante
Sous les arbres profonds et verts!

Elle faisait mon sort prospère,
Mon travail léger, mon ciel bleu.
Lorsqu'elle me disait: Mon père,
Tout mon cœur s'écriait: Mon Dieu!

A travers mes songes sans nombre,
J'écoutais son parler joyeux,
Et mon front s'éclairait dans l'ombre
A la lumière de ses yeux.

Elle avait l'air d'une princesse
Quand je la tenais par la main.
Elle cherchait des fleurs sans cesse
Et des pauvres dans le chemin.

Elle donnait comme on dérobe,
En se cachant aux yeux de tous.
Oh! la belle petite robe
Qu'elle avait, vous rappelez-vous?

Le soir, auprès de ma bougie,
Elle jasait à petit bruit,
Tandis qu'à la vitre rougie
Heurtaient les papillons de nuit.

Les anges se miraient en elle.
Que son bonjour était charmant!
Le ciel mettait dans sa prunelle
Ce regard qui jamais ne ment.

Oh! je l'avais, si jeune encore,
Vue apparaître en mon destin!
C'était l'enfant de mon aurore,
Et mon étoile du matin!

Quand la lune claire et sereine
Brillait aux cieux, dans ces beaux mois,
Comme nous allions dans la plaine!
Comme nous courions dans les bois!

Puis, vers la lumière isolée
Etoilant le logis obscur,
Nous revenions par la vallée
En tournant le coin du vieux mur;

Nous revenions, cœurs pleins de flamme,
En parlant des splendeurs du ciel.
Je composais cette jeune âme
Comme l'abeille fait son miel.

Doux ange aux candides pensées,
Elle était gaie en arrivant . . . –
Toutes ces choses sont passées
Comme l'ombre et comme le vent!

Villequier, 4 septembre 1844

Veni, vidi, vixi

J'ai bien assez vécu, puisque dans mes douleurs
Je marche sans trouver de bras qui me secourent,
Puisque je ris à peine aux enfants qui m'entourent,
Puisque je ne suis plus réjoui par les fleurs;

Puisqu'au printemps, quand Dieu met la nature en fête,
J'assiste, esprit sans joie, à ce splendide amour;
Puisque je suis à l'heure où l'homme fuit le jour,
Hélas! et sent de tout la tristesse secrète;

Puisque l'espoir serein dans mon âme est vaincu;
Puisqu'en cette saison des parfums et des roses,
O ma fille! j'aspire à l'ombre où tu reposes,
Puisque mon cœur est mort, j'ai bien assez vécu.

Je n'ai pas refusé ma tâche sur la terre.
Mon sillon? Le voilà. Ma gerbe? La voici.
J'ai vécu souriant, toujours plus adouci,
Debout, mais incliné du côté du mystère.

J'ai fait ce que j'ai pu; j'ai servi, j'ai veillé,
Et j'ai vu bien souvent qu'on riait de ma peine.
Je me suis étonné d'être un objet de haine,
Ayant beaucoup souffert et beaucoup travaillé.

Dans ce bagne terrestre où ne s'ouvre aucune aile,
Sans me plaindre, saignant, et tombant sur les mains,
Morne, épuisé, raillé par les forçats humains,
J'ai porté mon chaînon de la chaîne éternelle.

Maintenant, mon regard ne s'ouvre qu'à demi;
Je ne me tourne plus même quand on me nomme;
Je suis plein de stupeur et d'ennui, comme un homme
Qui se lève avant l'aube et qui n'a pas dormi.

Je ne daigne plus même, en ma sombre paresse,
Répondre à l'envieux dont la bouche me nuit.
O Seigneur! ouvrez-moi les portes de la nuit,
Afin que je m'en aille et que je disparaisse!

Avril 1848

'Demain, dès l'aube . . .'

Demain, dès l'aube, à l'heure où blanchit la campagne,
Je partirai. Vois-tu, je sais que tu m'attends.
J'irai par la forêt, j'irai par la montagne.
Je ne puis demeurer loin de toi plus longtemps.

Je marcherai les yeux fixés sur mes pensées,
Sans rien voir au dehors, sans entendre aucun bruit,
Seul, inconnu, le dos courbé, les mains croisées,
Triste, et le jour pour moi sera comme la nuit.

Je ne regarderai ni l'or du soir qui tombe,
Ni les voiles au loin descendant vers Harfleur,
Et quand j'arriverai, je mettrai sur ta tombe
Un bouquet de houx vert et de bruyère en fleur.

3 septembre 1847

Paroles sur la dune

Maintenant que mon temps décroît comme un flambeau,
    Que mes tâches sont terminées;
Maintenant que voici que je touche au tombeau
    Par les deuils et par les années,

Et qu'au fond de ce ciel que mon essor rêva,
    Je vois fuir, vers l'ombre entraînées,
Comme le tourbillon du passé qui s'en va,
    Tant de belles heures sonnées;

Maintenant que je dis: – Un jour, nous triomphons;
    Le lendemain, tout est mensonge! –
Je suis triste, et je marche au bord des flots profonds,
    Courbé comme celui qui songe.

Je regarde, au-dessus du mont et du vallon,
    Et des mers sans fin remuées,
S'envoler, sous le bec du vautour aquilon,
    Toute la toison des nuées;

J'entends le vent dans l'air, la mer sur le récif,
    L'homme liant la gerbe mûre;
J'écoute, et je confronte en mon esprit pensif
    Ce qui parle à ce qui murmure;

Et je reste parfois couché sans me lever
    Sur l'herbe rare de la dune,
Jusqu'à l'heure où l'on voit apparaître et rêver
    Les yeux sinistres de la lune.

Elle monte, elle jette un long rayon dormant
    A l'espace, au mystère, au gouffre;
Et nous nous regardons tous les deux fixement,
    Elle qui brille et moi qui souffre.

Où donc s'en sont allés mes jours évanouis?
    Est-il quelqu'un qui me connaisse?
Ai-je encor quelque chose en mes yeux éblouis,
    De la clarté de ma jeunesse?

Tout s'est-il envolé? Je suis seul, je suis las;
    J'appelle sans qu'on me réponde;
O vent! ô flots! ne suis-je aussi qu'un souffle, hélas!
    Hélas! ne suis-je aussi qu'une onde?

Ne verrai-je plus rien de tout ce que j'aimais?
    Au dedans de moi le soir tombe.
O terre, dont la brume efface les sommets,
    Suis-je le spectre, et toi la tombe?

Ai-je donc vidé tout, vie, amour, joie, espoir?
    J'attends, je demande, j'implore;
Je penche tour à tour mes urnes pour avoir
    De chacune une goutte encore!

Comme le souvenir est voisin du remord!
    Comme à pleurer tout nous ramène!
Et que je te sens froide en te touchant, ô mort,
    Noir verrou de la porte humaine!

Et je pense, écoutant gémir le vent amer,
    Et l'onde aux plis infranchissables;.
L'été rit, et l'on voit sur le bord de la mer
    Fleurir le chardon bleu des sables.

     5 août 1854, anniversaire de mon arrivée à Jersey

Pasteurs et troupeaux

à Madame Louise C.

Le vallon où je vais tous les jours est charmant,
Serein, abandonné, seul sous le firmament,
Plein de ronces en fleurs; c'est un sourire triste.
Il vous fait oublier que quelque chose existe,
Et, sans le bruit des champs remplis de travailleurs,
On ne saurait plus là si quelqu'un vit ailleurs.
Là, l'ombre fait l'amour; l'idylle naturelle
Rit; le bouvreuil avec le verdier s'y querelle,
Et la fauvette y met de travers son bonnet;
C'est tantôt l'aubépine et tantôt le genêt;
De noirs granits bourrus, puis des mousses riantes;
Car Dieu fait un poème avec des variantes;
Comme le vieil Homère, il rabâche parfois,
Mais c'est avec les fleurs, les monts, l'onde et les bois!
Une petite mare est là, ridant sa face,
Prenant des airs de flot pour la fourmi qui passe,

Ironie étalée au milieu du gazon,
Qu'ignore l'océan grondant à l'horizon.
J'y rencontre parfois sur la roche hideuse
Un doux être; quinze ans, yeux bleus, pieds nus, gardeuse
De chèvres, habitant, au fond d'un ravin noir,
Un vieux chaume croulant qui s'étoile le soir;
Ses sœurs sont au logis et filent leur quenouille;
Elle essuie aux roseaux ses pieds que l'étang mouille;
Chèvres, brebis, béliers, paissent; quand, sombre esprit,
J'apparais, le pauvre ange a peur, et me sourit;
Et moi, je la salue, elle étant l'innocence.
Ses agneaux, dans le pré plein de fleurs qui l'encense,
Bondissent, et chacun, au soleil s'empourprant,
Laisse aux buissons, à qui la bise le reprend,
Un peu de sa toison, comme un flocon d'écume.
Je passe; enfant, troupeau, s'effacent dans la brume;
Le crépuscule étend sur les longs sillons gris
Ses ailes de fantôme et de chauve-souris;
J'entends encore au loin dans la plaine ouvrière
Chanter derrière moi la douce chevrière,
Et, là-bas, devant moi, le vieux gardien pensif
De l'écume, du flot, de l'algue, du récif,
Et des vagues sans trêve et sans fin remuées,
Le pâtre promontoire au chapeau de nuées,
S'accoude et rêve au bruit de tous les infinis,
Et, dans l'ascension des nuages bénis,
Regarde se lever la lune triomphale,
Pendant que l'ombre tremble, et que l'âpre rafale
Disperse à tous les vents avec son souffle amer
La laine des moutons sinistres de la mer.

Jersey, Grouville, avril 1855

Ce que c'est que la mort

Ne dites pas: mourir; dites: naître. Croyez.
On voit ce que je vois et ce que vous voyez;
On est l'homme mauvais que je suis, que vous êtes;
On se rue aux plaisirs, aux tourbillons, aux fêtes;
On tâche d'oublier le bas, la fin, l'écueil,
La sombre égalité du mal et du cercueil;
Quoique le plus petit vaille le plus prospère;
Car tous les hommes sont les fils du même père,
Ils sont la même larme et sortent du même œil.
On vit, usant ses jours à se remplir d'orgueil;
On marche, on court, on rêve, on souffre, on penche, on tombe,
On monte. Quelle est donc cette aube? C'est la tombe.
Où suis-je? Dans la mort. Viens! Un vent inconnu
Vous jette au seuil des cieux. On tremble; on se voit nu,
Impur, hideux, noué des mille nœuds funèbres
De ses torts, de ses maux honteux, de ses ténèbres;
Et soudain on entend quelqu'un dans l'infini
Qui chante, et par quelqu'un on sent qu'on est béni,
Sans voir la main d'où tombe à notre âme méchante
L'amour, et sans savoir quelle est la voix qui chante.
On arrive homme, deuil, glaçon, neige; on se sent
Fondre et vivre; et, d'extase et d'azur s'emplissant,
Tout notre être frémit de la défaite étrange
Du monstre qui devient dans la lumière un ange.

Au dolmen de la tour Blanche, jour des Morts, novembre 1854

Nomen, numen, lumen

Quand il eut terminé, quand les soleils épars,
Eblouis, du chaos montant de toutes parts,
Se furent tous rangés à leur place profonde,
Il sentit le besoin de se nommer au monde;
Et l'être formidable et serein se leva;
Il se dressa sur l'ombre et cria: JÉHOVAH!
Et dans l'immensité ces sept lettres tombèrent;
Et ce sont, dans les cieux que nos yeux réverbèrent,
Au-dessus de nos fronts tremblants sous leur rayon,
Les sept astres géants du noir septentrion.

Minuit, au dolmen du Faldouet, 1er mars 1855

[pp. 105–106]

Le sacre de la femme

I

L'aurore apparaissait; quelle aurore? Un abîme
D'éblouissement, vaste, insondable, sublime;
Une ardente lueur de paix et de bonté.
C'était aux premiers temps du globe; et la clarté
Brillait sereine au front du ciel inaccessible,
Étant tout ce que Dieu peut avoir de visible;
Tout s'illuminait, l'ombre et le brouillard obscur;
Des avalanches d'or s'écroulaient dans l'azur;
Le jour en flamme, au fond de la terre ravie,
Embrasait les lointains splendides de la vie;
Les horizons, pleins d'ombre et de rocs chevelus
Et d'arbres effrayants que l'homme ne voit plus,
Luisaient, comme le songe et comme le vertige,
Dans une profondeur d'éclair et de prodige;
L'éden pudique et nu s'éveillait mollement;
Les oiseaux gazouillaient un hymne si charmant,
Si frais, si gracieux, si suave et si tendre,
Que les anges distraits se penchaient pour l'entendre;
Le seul rugissement du tigre était plus doux;
Les halliers où l'agneau paissait avec les loups,
Les mers où l'hydre aimait l'alycon, et les plaines
Où les ours et les daims confondaient leurs haleines,
Hésitaient, dans le chœur des concerts infinis,
Entre le cri de l'antre et la chanson des nids.
La prière semblait à la clarté mêlée;
Et sur cette nature encore immaculée
Qui du verbe éternel avait gardé l'accent,
Sur ce monde céleste, angélique, innocent,
Le matin, murmurant une sainte parole,
Souriait, et l'aurore était une auréole.
Tout avait la figure intègre du bonheur;
Pas de bouche d'où vînt un souffle empoisonneur;
Pas un être qui n'eût sa majesté première;
Tout ce que l'infini peut jeter de lumière
Éclatait pêle-mêle à la fois dans les airs;
Le vent jouait avec cette gerbe d'éclairs
Dans le tourbillon libre et fuyant des nuées;
L'enfer balbutiait quelques vagues huées
Qui s'évanouissaient dans le grand cri joyeux
Des eaux, des monts, des bois, de la terre et des cieux!
Les vents et les rayons semaient de tels délires
Que les forêts vibraient comme de grandes lyres;
De l'ombre à la clarté, de la base au sommet,
Une fraternité vénérable germait;

L'astre était sans orgueil et le ver sans envie;
On s'adorait d'un bout à l'autre de la vie:
Une harmonie égale à la clarté, versant
Une extase divine au globe adolescent,
Semblait sortir du cœur mystérieux du monde;
L'herbe en était émue, et le nuage, et l'onde,
Et même le rocher qui songe et qui se tait;
L'arbre, tout pénétré de lumière, chantait;
Chaque fleur, échangeant son souffle et sa pensée
Avec le ciel serein d'où tombe la rosée,
Recevait une perle et donnait un parfum;
L'Être resplendissait, Un dans Tout, Tout dans Un;
Le paradis brillait sous les sombres ramures
De la vie ivre d'ombre et pleine de murmures,
Et la lumière était faite de vérité;
Et tout avait la grâce, ayant la pureté;
Tout était flamme, hymen, bonheur, douceur, clémence,
Tant ces immenses jours avaient une aube immense!

II

Ineffable lever du premier rayon d'or,
Du jour éclairant tout sans rien savoir encor!
O matin des matins! amour! joie effrénée
De commencer le temps, l'heure, le mois, l'année!
Ouverture du monde! instant prodigieux!
La nuit se dissolvait dans les énormes cieux
Où rien ne tremble, où rien ne pleure, où rien ne souffre;
Autant que le chaos la lumière était gouffre;
Dieu se manifestait dans sa calme grandeur,
Certitude pour l'âme et pour les yeux splendeur;
De faîte en faîte, au ciel et sur terre, et dans toutes
Les épaisseurs de l'être aux innombrables voûtes,
On voyait l'évidence adorable éclater;
Le monde s'ébauchait; tout semblait méditer;
Les types primitifs, offrant dans leur mélange
Presque la brute informe et rude et presque l'ange,
Surgissaient, orageux, gigantesques, touffus;
On sentait tressaillir sous leurs groupes confus
La terre, inépuisable et suprême matrice;
La création sainte, à son tour créatrice,
Modelait vaguement des aspects merveilleux,
Faisait sortir l'essaim des êtres fabuleux
Tantôt des bois, tantôt des mers, tantôt des nues,
Et proposait à Dieu des formes inconnues
Que le temps, moissonneur pensif, plus tard changea;
On sentait sourdre, et vivre, et végéter déjà
Tous les arbres futurs, pins, érables, yeuses,
Dans des verdissements de feuilles monstrueuses;

Une sorte de vie excessive gonflait
La mamelle du monde au mystérieux lait;
Tout semblait presque hors de la mesure éclore;
Comme si la nature, en étant proche encore,
Eût pris, pour ses essais sur la terre et les eaux,
Une difformité splendide au noir chaos.

Les divins paradis, pleins d'une étrange sève,
Semblent au fond des temps reluire dans le rêve,
Et pour nos yeux obscurs, sans idéal, sans foi,
Leur extase aujourd'hui serait presque l'effroi;
Mais qu'importe à l'abîme, à l'âme universelle
Qui dépense un soleil au lieu d'une étincelle,
Et qui, pour y pouvoir poser l'ange azuré,
Fait croître jusqu'aux cieux l'Éden démesuré!

Jours inouïs! le bien, le beau, le vrai, le juste
Coulaient dans le torrent, frissonnaient dans l'arbuste;
L'aquilon louait Dieu de sagesse vêtu;
L'arbre était bon; la fleur était une vertu;
C'est trop peu d'être blanc, le lys était candide;
Rien n'avait de souillure et rien n'avait de ride;
Jours purs! rien ne saignait sous l'ongle et sous la dent;
La bête heureuse était l'innocence rôdant;
Le mal n'avait encor rien mis de son mystère
Dans le serpent, dans l'aigle altier, dans la panthère;
Le précipice ouvert dans l'animal sacré
N'avait pas d'ombre, étant jusqu'au fond éclairé;
La montagne était jeune et la vague était vierge;
Le globe, hors des mers dont le flot le submerge,
Sortait beau, magnifique, aimant, fier, triomphant,
Et rien n'était petit quoique tout fût enfant;
La terre avait, parmi ses hymnes d'innocence,
Un étourdissement de sève et de croissance;
L'instinct fécond faisait rêver l'instinct vivant;
Et, répandu partout, sur les eaux, dans le vent,
L'amour épars flottait comme un parfum s'exhale;
La nature riait, naïve et colossale;
L'espace vagissait ainsi qu'un nouveau-né.
L'aube était le regard du soleil étonné.

III

Or, ce jour-là, c'était le plus beau qu'eût encore
Versé sur l'univers la radieuse aurore;
Le même séraphique et saint frémissement
Unissait l'algue à l'onde et l'être à l'élément;
L'éther plus pur luisait dans les cieux plus sublimes;
Les souffles abondaient plus profonds sur les cimes;

Les feuillages avaient de plus doux mouvements;
Et les rayons tombaient caressants et charmants
Sur un frais vallon vert, où, débordant d'extase,
Adorant ce grand ciel que la lumière embrase,
Heureux d'être, joyeux d'aimer, ivres de voir,
Dans l'ombre, au bord d'un lac, vertigineux miroir,
Étaient assis, les pieds effleurés par la lame,
Le premier homme auprès de la première femme.

L'époux priait, ayant l'épouse à son côté.

IV

Ève offrait au ciel bleu la sainte nudité;
Ève blonde admirait l'aube, sa sœur vermeille.

Chair de la femme! argile idéale! ô merveille!
O pénétration sublime de l'esprit
Dans le limon que l'Être ineffable pétrit!
Matière où l'âme brille à travers son suaire!
Boue où l'on voit les doigts du divin statuaire!
Fange auguste appelant le baiser et le cœur,
Si sainte, qu'on ne sait, tant l'amour est vainqueur,
Tant l'âme est vers ce lit mystérieux poussée,
Si cette volupté n'est pas une pensée,
Et qu'on ne peut, à l'heure où les sens sont en feu,
Étreindre la beauté sans croire embrasser Dieu!

Ève laissait errer ses yeux sur la nature.

Et, sous les verts palmiers à la haute stature,
Autour d'Ève, au-dessus de sa tête, l'œillet
Semblait songer, le bleu lotus se recueillait,
Le frais myosotis se souvenait; les roses
Cherchaient ses pieds avec leurs lèvres demi-closes;
Un souffle fraternel sortait du lys vermeil;
Comme si ce doux être eût été leur pareil,
Comme si de ces fleurs, ayant toutes une âme,
La plus belle s'était épanouie en femme.

V

Pourtant, jusqu'à ce jour, c'était Adam, l'élu
Qui dans le ciel sacré le premier avait lu,
C'était le Marié tranquille et fort, que l'ombre
Et la lumière, et l'aube, et les astres sans nombre,
Et les bêtes des bois, et les fleurs du ravin
Suivaient ou vénéraient comme l'aîné divin,
Comme le front ayant la lueur la plus haute;
Et, quand tous deux, la main dans la main, côte à côte,

Erraient dans la clarté de l'Éden radieux,
La nature sans fond, sous ses millions d'yeux,
A travers les rochers, les rameaux, l'onde et l'herbe,
Couvait, avec amour pour le couple superbe,
Avec plus de respect pour l'homme, être complet,
Ève qui regardait, Adam qui contemplait.
Mais, ce jour-là, ces yeux innombrables qu'entr'ouvre
L'infini sous les plis du voile qui le couvre,
S'attachaient sur l'épouse et non pas sur l'époux,
Comme si, dans ce jour religieux et doux,
Béni parmi les jours et parmi les aurores,
Aux nids ailés perdus sous les branches sonores,
Au nuage, aux ruisseaux, aux frissonnants essaims,
Aux bêtes, aux cailloux, à tous ces êtres saints
Que de mots ténébreux la terre aujourd'hui nomme,
La femme eût apparu plus auguste que l'homme!

VI

Pourquoi ce choix? pourquoi cet attendrissement
Immense du profond et divin firmament?
Pourquoi tout l'univers penché sur une tête?
Pourquoi l'aube donnant à la femme une fête?
Pourquoi ces chants? Pourquoi ces palpitations
Des flots dans plus de joie et dans plus de rayons?
Pourquoi partout l'ivresse et la hâte d'éclore,
Et les antres heureux de s'ouvrir à l'aurore,
Et plus d'encens sur terre et plus de flamme aux cieux?

Le beau couple innocent songeait silencieux.

VII

Cependant la tendresse inexprimable et douce
De l'astre, du vallon, du lac, du brin de mousse,
Tressaillait plus profonde à chaque instant autour
D'Ève, que saluait du haut des cieux le jour;
Le regard qui sortait des choses et des êtres,
Des flots bénis, des bois sacrés, des arbres prêtres,
Se fixait, plus pensif de moment en moment,
Sur cette femme au front vénérable et charmant;
Un long rayon d'amour lui venait des abîmes,
De l'ombre, de l'azur, des profondeurs, des cimes,
De la fleur, de l'oiseau chantant, du roc muet.

Et, pâle, Ève sentit que son flanc remuait.

5–17 octobre 1858

La conscience

Lorsque avec ses enfants vêtus de peaux de bêtes,
Échevelé, livide au milieu des tempêtes,
Caïn se fut enfui de devant Jéhovah,
Comme le soir tombait, l'homme sombre arriva
Au bas d'une montagne en une grande plaine;
Sa femme fatiguée et ses fils hors d'haleine
Lui dirent: «Couchons-nous sur la terre, et dormons.»
Caïn, ne dormant pas, songeait au pied des monts.
Ayant levé la tête, au fond des cieux funèbres
Il vit un œil, tout grand ouvert dans les ténèbres,
Et qui le regardait dans l'ombre fixement.
«Je suis trop près», dit-il avec un tremblement.
Il réveilla ses fils dormant, sa femme lasse,
Et se remit à fuir sinistre dans l'espace.
Il marcha trente jours, il marcha trente nuits.
Il allait, muet, pâle et fremissant aux bruits,
Furtif, sans regarder derrière lui, sans trêve,
Sans repos, sans sommeil; il atteignit la grève
Des mers dans le pays qui fut depuis Assur.
«Arrêtons-nous, dit-il, car cet asile est sûr.
Restons-y. Nous avons du monde atteint les bornes.»
Et, comme il s'asseyait, il vit dans les cieux mornes
L'œil à la même place au fond de l'horizon.
Alors il tressaillit en proie au noir frisson.
«Cachez-moi!» cria-t-il; et, le doigt sur la bouche,
Tous ses fils regardaient trembler l'aïeul farouche.
Caïn dit à Jabel, père de ceux qui vont
Sous des tentes de poil dans le désert profond:
«Étends de ce côté la toile de la tente.»
Et l'on développa la muraille flottante;
Et, quand on l'eut fixée avec des poids de plomb:
«Vous ne voyez plus rien?» dit Tsilla, l'enfant blond,
La fille de ses fils, douce comme l'aurore;
Et Caïn répondit: «Je vois cet œil encore!»
Jubal, père de ceux qui passent dans les bourgs
Soufflant dans des clairons et frappant des tambours,
Cria: «Je saurai bien construire une barrière.»
Il fit un mur de bronze et mit Caïn derrière.
Et Caïn dit: «Cet œil me regarde toujours!»
Hénoch dit: «Il faut faire une enceinte de tours
Si terrible, que rien ne puisse approcher d'elle.
Bâtissons une ville avec sa citadelle.
Bâtissons une ville, et nous la fermerons.»
Alors Tubalcaïn, père des forgerons,

Construisit une ville énorme et surhumaine.
Pendant qu'il travaillait, ses frères, dans la plaine,
Chassaient les fils d'Énos et les enfants de Seth;
Et l'on crevait les yeux à quiconque passait;
Et, le soir, on lançait des flèches aux étoiles.
Le granit remplaça la tente aux murs de toiles,
On lia chaque bloc avec des nœuds de fer,
Et la ville semblait une ville d'enfer;
L'ombre des tours faisait la nuit dans les campagnes;
Ils donnèrent aux murs l'épaisseur des montagnes;
Sur la porte on grava: «Défense à Dieu d'entrer.»
Quand ils eurent fini de clore et de murer,
On mit l'aïeul au centre en une tour de pierre;
Et lui restait lugubre et hagard. «O mon père!
L'œil a-t-il disparu?» dit en tremblant Tsilla.
Et Caïn répondit: «Non, il est toujours là.»
Alors il dit: «Je veux habiter sous la terre
Comme dans son sépulcre un homme solitaire;
Rien ne me verra plus, je ne verrai plus rien.»
On fit donc une fosse, et Caïn dit: «C'est bien!»
Puis il descendit seul sous cette voûte sombre.
Quand il se fut assis sur sa chaise dans l'ombre
Et qu'on eut sur son front fermé le souterrain,
L'œil était dans la tombe et regardait Caïn.

Booz endormi

Booz s'était couché de fatigue accablé;
Il avait tout le jour travaillé dans son aire,
Puis avait fait son lit à sa place ordinaire;
Booz dormait auprès des boisseaux pleins de blé.

Ce vieillard possédait des champs de blés et d'orge;
Il était, quoique riche, à la justice enclin;
Il n'avait pas de fange en l'eau de son moulin;
Il n'avait pas d'enfer dans le feu de sa forge.

Sa barbe était d'argent comme un ruisseau d'avril.
Sa gerbe n'était point avare ni haineuse;
Quand il voyait passer quelque pauvre glaneuse:
«Laissez tomber exprès des épis», disait-il.

Cet homme marchait pur loin des sentiers obliques,
Vêtu de probité candide et de lin blanc;
Et, toujours du côté des pauvres ruisselant,
Ses sacs de grains semblaient des fontaines publiques.

Booz était bon maître et fidèle parent;
Il était généreux, quoiqu'il fût économe;
Les femmes regardaient Booz plus qu'un jeune homme,
Car le jeune homme est beau, mais le vieillard est grand.

Le vieillard, qui revient vers la source première,
Entre aux jours éternels et sort des jours changeants;
Et l'on voit de la flamme aux yeux des jeunes gens,
Mais dans l'œil du vieillard on voit de la lumière.

                        *

Donc, Booz dans la nuit dormait parmi les siens.
Près des meules, qu'on eût prises pour des décombres,
Les moissonneurs couchés faisaient des groupes sombres;
Et ceci se passait dans des temps très anciens.

Les tribus d'Israël avaient pour chef un juge;
La terre, où l'homme errait sous la tente, inquiet
Des empreintes de pieds de géant qu'il voyait,
Était mouillée encor et molle du déluge.

                        *

Comme dormait Jacob, comme dormait Judith,
Booz, les yeux fermés, gisait sous la feuillée;
Or, la porte du ciel s'étant entre-bâillée
Au-dessus de sa tête, un songe en descendit.

Et ce songe était tel, que Booz vit un chêne
Qui, sorti de son ventre, allait jusqu'au ciel bleu;
Une race y montait comme une longue chaîne;
Un roi chantait en bas, en haut mourait un Dieu.

Et Booz murmurait avec la voix de l'âme:
«Comment se pourrait-il que de moi ceci vînt?
Le chiffre de mes ans a passé quatrevingt,
Et je n'ai pas de fils, et je n'ai plus de femme.

«Voilà longtemps que celle avec qui j'ai dormi,
O Seigneur! a quitté ma couche pour la vôtre;
Et nous sommes encor tout mêlés l'un à l'autre,
Elle à demi vivante et moi mort à demi.

«Une race naîtrait de moi! Comment le croire?
Comment se pourrait-il que j'eusse des enfants?
Quand on est jeune, on a des matins triomphants;
Le jour sort de la nuit comme d'une victoire;

«Mais vieux, on tremble ainsi qu'à l'hiver le bouleau;
Je suis veuf, je suis seul, et sur moi le soir tombe,
Et je courbe, ô mon Dieu! mon âme vers la tombe,
Comme un bœuf ayant soif penche son front vers l'eau.»

Ainsi parlait Booz dans le rêve et l'extase,
Tournant vers Dieu ses yeux par le sommeil noyés;
Le cèdre ne sent pas une rose à sa base,
Et lui ne sentait pas une femme à ses pieds.

    *

Pendant qu'il sommeillait, Ruth, une moabite,
S'était couchée aux pieds de Booz, le sein nu,
Espérant on ne sait quel rayon inconnu
Quand viendrait du réveil la lumière subite.

Booz ne savait point qu'une femme était là,
Et Ruth ne savait point ce que Dieu voulait d'elle.
Un frais parfum sortait des touffes d'asphodèle;
Les souffles de la nuit flottaient sur Galgala.

L'ombre était nuptiale, auguste et solennelle;
Les anges y volaient sans doute obscurément,
Car on voyait passer dans la nuit, par moment,
Quelque chose de bleu qui paraissait une aile.

La respiration de Booz qui dormait
Se mêlait au bruit sourd des ruisseaux sur la mousse.
On était dans le mois où la nature est douce,
Les collines ayant des lys sur leur sommet.

Ruth songeait et Booz dormait; l'herbe était noire;
Les grelots des troupeaux palpitaient vaguement;
Une immense bonté tombait du firmament;
C'était l'heure tranquille où les lions vont boire.

Tout reposait dans Ur et dans Jérimadeth;
Les astres émaillaient le ciel profond et sombre;
Le croissant fin et clair parmi ces fleurs de l'ombre
Brillait à l'occident, et Ruth se demandait,

Immobile, ouvrant l'œil à moitié sous ses voiles,
Quel dieu, quel moissonneur de l'éternel été,
Avait, en s'en allant, négligemment jeté
Cette faucille d'or dans le champ des étoiles.

1ᵉʳ mai 1859

Première rencontre du Christ avec le tombeau

En ce temps-là, Jésus était dans la Judée;
Il avait délivré la femme possédée,
Rendu l'ouïe aux sourds et guéri les lépreux;
Les prêtres l'épiaient et parlaient bas entre eux.
Comme il s'en retournait vers la ville bénie,
Lazare, homme de bien, mourut à Béthanie.
Marthe et Marie étaient ses sœurs; Marie, un jour,
Pour laver les pieds nus du maître plein d'amour,
Avait été chercher son parfum le plus rare.
Or, Jésus aimait Marthe et Marie et Lazare.
Quelqu'un lui dit: « Lazare est mort.»

                      Le lendemain,
Comme le peuple était venu sur son chemin,
Il expliquait la loi, les livres, les symboles,
Et, comme Élie et Job, parlait par paraboles.
Il disait: «Qui me suit, aux anges est pareil.
Quand un homme a marché tout le jour au soleil
Dans un chemin sans puits et sans hôtellerie,
S'il ne croit pas, quand vient le soir, il pleure, il crie,
Il est las; sur la terre il tombe haletant.
S'il croit en moi, qu'il prie, il peut au même instant
Continuer sa route avec des forces triples.»
Puis il s'interrompit, et dit à ses disciples:
«Lazare, notre ami, dort; je vais l'éveiller.»
Eux dirent: «Nous irons, maître, où tu veux aller.»
Or, de Jérusalem, où Salomon mit l'arche,
Pour gagner Béthanie, il faut trois jours de marche.
Jésus partit. Durant cette route souvent,
Tandis qu'il marchait seul et pensif en avant,
Son vêtement parut blanc comme la lumière.

Quand Jésus arriva, Marthe vint la première,
Et, tombant à ses pieds, s'écria tout d'abord:

[*pp.* 119–120]

«Si nous t'avions eu, maître, il ne serait pas mort.»
Puis reprit en pleurant: «Mais il a rendu l'âme.
Tu viens trop tard.» Jésus lui dit: «Qu'en sais-tu, femme?
Le moissonneur est seul maître de la moisson.»

Marie était restée assise à la maison.

Marthe lui cria: «Viens, le maître te réclame.»
Elle vint. Jésus dit: «Pourquoi pleures-tu, femme?»
Et Marie à genoux lui dit: «Toi seul es fort.
Si nous t'avions eu, maître, il ne serait pas mort.»
Jésus reprit: «Je suis la lumière et la vie.
Heureux celui qui voit ma trace et l'a suivie!
Qui croit en moi vivra, fût-il mort et gisant.»
Et Thomas, appelé Didyme, était présent.

Et le Seigneur, dont Jean et Pierre suivaient l'ombre,
Dit aux juifs accourus pour le voir en grand nombre:
«Où donc l'avez-vous mis?» Ils répondirent: «Vois»,
Lui montrant de la main, dans un champ, près d'un bois,
A côté d'un torrent qui dans les pierres coule,
Un sépulcre.

                    Et Jésus pleura.

                              Sur quoi la foule
Se prit à s'écrier: «Voyez comme il l'aimait!
Lui qui chasse, dit-on, Satan et le soumet,
Eût-il, s'il était Dieu, comme on nous le rapporte,
Laissé mourir quelqu'un qu'il aimait de la sorte?»

Or, Marthe conduisit au sépulcre Jésus.
Il vint. On avait mis une pierre dessus.
«Je crois en vous, dit Marthe, ainsi que Jean et Pierre;
Mais voilà quatre jours qu'il est sous cette pierre.»

Et Jésus dit: «Tais-toi, femme, car c'est le lieu
Où tu vas, si tu crois, voir la gloire de Dieu.»
Puis il reprit: «Il faut que cette pierre tombe.»
La pierre ôtée, on vit le dedans de la tombe.

Jésus leva les yeux au ciel et marcha seul
Vers cette ombre où le mort gisait dans son linceul,
Pareil au sac d'argent qu'enfouit un avare.
Et, se penchant, il dit à haute voix: «Lazare!»

Alors le mort sortit du sépulcre; ses pieds
Des bandes du linceul étaient encor liés;

Il se dressa debout le long de la muraille;
Jésus dit: «Déliez cet homme, et qu'il s'en aille.»
Ceux qui virent cela crurent en Jésus-Christ.

Or, les prêtres, selon qu'au livre il est écrit,
S'assemblèrent, troublés, chez le préteur de Rome;
Sachant que Christ avait ressuscité cet homme,
Et que tous avaient vu le sépulcre s'ouvrir,
Ils dirent: «Il est temps de le faire mourir.»

Jersey. 23 octobre 1852

La rose de l'infante

Elle est toute petite; une duègne la garde.
Elle tient à la main une rose et regarde.
Quoi? que regarde-t-elle? Elle ne sait pas. L'eau;
Un bassin qu'assombrit le pin et le bouleau;
Ce qu'elle a devant elle; un cygne aux ailes blanches,
Le bercement des flots sous la chanson des branches,
Et le profond jardin rayonnant et fleuri.
Tout ce bel ange a l'air dans la neige pétri.
On voit un grand palais comme au fond d'une gloire,
Un parc, de clairs viviers où les biches vont boire,
Et des paons étoilés sous les bois chevelus.
L'innocence est sur elle une blancheur de plus;
Toutes ses grâces font comme un faisceau qui tremble.
Autour de cette enfant l'herbe est splendide et semble
Pleine de vrais rubis et de diamants fins;
Un jet de saphirs sort des bouches des dauphins.
Elle se tient au bord de l'eau; sa fleur l'occupe;
Sa basquine est en point de Gênes; sur sa jupe
Une arabesque, errant dans les plis du satin,
Suit les mille détours d'un fil d'or florentin.
La rose épanouie et toute grande ouverte,
Sortant du frais bouton comme d'une urne verte,
Charge la petitesse exquise de sa main;
Quand l'enfant, allongeant ses lèvres de carmin,
Fronce, en la respirant, sa riante narine,
La magnifique fleur, royale et purpurine,
Cache plus qu'à demi ce visage charmant,
Si bien que l'œil hésite, et qu'on ne sait comment
Distinguer de la fleur ce bel enfant qui joue,

Et si l'on voit la rose ou si l'on voit la joue.
Ses yeux bleus sont plus beaux sous son pur sourcil brun.
En elle tout est joie, enchantement, parfum;
Quel doux regard, l'azur! et quel doux nom, Marie!
Tout est rayon; son œil éclaire et son nom prie.
Pourtant, devant la vie et sous le firmament,
Pauvre être! elle se sent très grande vaguement;
Elle assiste au printemps, à la lumière, à l'ombre,
Au grand soleil couchant horizontal et sombre,
A la magnificence éclatante du soir,
Aux ruisseaux murmurants qu'on entend sans les voir,
Aux champs, à la nature éternelle et sereine,
Avec la gravité d'une petite reine;
Elle n'a jamais vu l'homme que se courbant;
Elle gouvernera la Flandre ou la Sardaigne.
Elle est l'infante, elle a cinq ans, elle dédaigne.
Car les enfants des rois sont ainsi; leurs fronts blancs
Portent un cercle d'ombre, et leurs pas chancelants
Sont des commencements de règne. Elle respire
Sa fleur en attendant qu'on lui cueille un empire;
Et son regard, déjà royal, dit: C'est à moi.
Il sort d'elle un amour mêlé d'un vague effroi.
Si quelqu'un, la voyant si tremblante et si frêle,
Fût-ce pour la sauver, mettait la main sur elle,
Avant qu'il eût pu faire un pas ou dire un mot,
Il aurait sur le front l'ombre de l'échafaud.

La douce enfant sourit, ne faisant autre chose
Que de vivre et d'avoir dans la main une rose,
Et d'être là devant le ciel, parmi les fleurs.

Le jour s'éteint; les nids chuchotent, querelleurs;
Les pourpres du couchant sont dans les branches d'arbre;
La rougeur monte au front des déesses de marbre
Qui semblent palpiter sentant venir la nuit;
Et tout ce qui planait redescend; plus de bruit,
Plus de flamme; le soir mystérieux recueille
Le soleil sous la vague et l'oiseau sous la feuille.

Pendant que l'enfant rit, cette fleur à la main,
Dans le vaste palais catholique romain
Dont chaque ogive semble au soleil une mitre,
Quelqu'un de formidable est derrière la vitre;
On voit d'en bas une ombre, au fond d'une vapeur,
De fenêtre en fenêtre errer, et l'on a peur;
Cette ombre au même endroit, comme en un cimetière,
Parfois est immobile une journée entière;
C'est un être effrayant qui semble ne rien voir;

Il rôde d'une chambre à l'autre, pâle et noir;
Il colle aux vitraux blancs son front lugubre, et songe;
Spectre blême! Son ombre aux feux du soir s'allonge;
Son pas funèbre est lent comme un glas de beffroi;
Et c'est la Mort, à moins que ce ne soit le Roi.

C'est lui; l'homme en qui vit et tremble le royaume.
Si quelqu'un pouvait voir dans l'œil de ce fantôme
Debout en ce moment l'épaule contre un mur,
Ce qu'on apercevrait dans cet abîme obscur,
Ce n'est pas l'humble enfant, le jardin, l'eau moirée
Reflétant le ciel d'or d'une claire soirée,
Les bosquets, les oiseaux se becquetant entre eux,
Non: au fond de cet œil comme l'onde vitreux,
Sous ce fatal sourcil qui dérobe à la sonde
Cette prunelle autant que l'océan profonde,
Ce qu'on distinguerait, c'est, mirage mouvant,
Tout un vol de vaisseaux en fuite dans le vent,
Et dans l'écume, au pli des vagues, sous l'étoile,
L'immense tremblement d'une flotte à la voile,
Et, là-bas, sous la brume, une île, un blanc rocher,
Écoutant sur les flots ces tonnerres marcher.

Telle est la vision qui, dans l'heure où nous sommes,
Emplit le froid cerveau de ce maître des hommes,
Et qui fait qu'il ne peut rien voir autour de lui.
L'armada, formidable et flottant point d'appui
Du levier dont il va soulever tout un monde,
Traverse en ce moment l'obscurité de l'onde;
Le roi dans son esprit la suit des yeux, vainqueur,
Et son tragique ennui n'a plus d'autre lueur.

Philippe Deux était une chose terrible.
Iblis dans le Koran et Caïn dans la Bible
Sont à peine aussi noirs qu'en son Escurial
Ce royal spectre, fils du spectre impérial.
Philippe Deux était le Mal tenant le glaive.
Il occupait le haut du monde comme un rêve.
Il vivait: nul n'osait le regarder; l'effroi
Faisait une lumière étrange autour du roi;
On tremblait rien qu'à voir passer ses majordomes;
Tant il se confondait, aux yeux troubles des hommes,
Avec l'abîme, avec les astres du ciel bleu!
Tant semblait grande à tous son approche de Dieu!
Sa volonté fatale, enfoncée, obstinée,
Était comme un crampon mis sur la destinée;
Il tenait l'Amérique et l'Inde, il s'appuyait
Sur l'Afrique, il régnait sur l'Europe, inquiet

Seulement du côté de la sombre Angleterre;
Sa bouche était silence et son âme mystère;
Son trône était de piège et de fraude construit;
Il avait pour soutien la force de la nuit;
L'ombre était le cheval de sa statue équestre.
Toujours vêtu de noir, ce Tout-Puissant terrestre
Avait l'air d'être en deuil de ce qu'il existait;
Il ressemblait au sphinx qui digère et se tait;
Immuable; étant tout, il n'avait rien à dire.
Nul n'avait vu ce roi sourire; le sourire
N'étant pas plus possible à ces lèvres de fer
Que l'aurore à la grille obscure de l'enfer.
S'il secouait parfois sa torpeur de couleuvre,
C'était pour assister le bourreau dans son œuvre,
Et sa prunelle avait pour clarté le reflet
Des bûchers sur lesquels par moments il soufflait.
Il était redoutable à la pensée, à l'homme,
A la vie, au progrès, au droit, dévot à Rome;
C'était Satan régnant au nom de Jésus-Christ;
Les choses qui sortaient de son nocturne esprit
Semblaient un glissement sinistre de vipères.
L'Escurial, Burgos, Aranjuez, ses repaires,
Jamais n'illuminaient leurs livides plafonds;
Pas de festins, jamais de cour, pas de bouffons;
Les trahisons pour jeu, l'autodafé pour fête.
Les rois troublés avaient au-dessus de leur tête
Ses projets dans la nuit obscurément ouverts;
Sa rêverie était un poids sur l'univers;
Il pouvait et voulait tout vaincre et tout dissoudre;
Sa prière faisait le bruit sourd d'une foudre;
De grands éclairs sortaient de ses songes profonds.
Ceux auxquels il pensait disaient: Nous étouffons.
Et les peuples, d'un bout à l'autre de l'empire,
Tremblaient, sentant sur eux ces deux yeux fixes luire.

Charles fut le vautour, Philippe est le hibou.

Morne en son noir pourpoint, la toison d'or au cou,
On dirait du destin la froide sentinelle;
Son immobilité commande; sa prunelle
Luit comme un soupirail de caverne; son doigt
Semble, ébauchant un geste obscur que nul ne voit,
Donner un ordre à l'ombre et vaguement l'écrire.
Chose inouïe! il vient de grincer un sourire.
Un sourire insondable, impénétrable, amer.
C'est que la vision de son armée en mer
Grandit de plus en plus dans sa sombre pensée;
C'est qu'il la voit voguer par son dessein poussée,

Comme s'il était là, planant sous le zénith;
Tout est bien; l'océan docile s'aplanit;
L'armada lui fait peur comme au déluge l'arche;
La flotte se déploie en bon ordre de marche,
Et, les vaisseaux gardant les espaces fixés,
Échiquier de tillacs, de ponts, de mâts dressés,
Ondule sur les eaux comme une immense claie.
Ces vaisseaux sont sacrés; les flots leur font la haie;
Les courants, pour aider ces nefs à débarquer,
Ont leur besogne à faire et n'y sauraient manquer;
Autour d'elles la vague avec amour déferle,
L'écueil se change en port, l'écume tombe en perle.
Voici chaque galère avec son gastadour;
Voilà ceux de l'Escaut, voilà ceux de l'Adour;
Les cent mestres de camp et les deux connétables;
L'Allemagne a donné ses ourques redoutables,
Naples ses brigantins, Cadix ses galions,
Lisbonne ses marins, car il faut des lions.
Et Philippe se penche, et, qu'importe l'espace?
Non seulement il voit, mais il entend. On passe,
On court, on va. Voici le cri des porte-voix,
Le pas des matelots courant sur les pavois,
Les moços, l'amiral appuyé sur son page,
Les tambours, les sifflets des maîtres d'équipage,
Les signaux pour la mer, l'appel pour les combats,
Le fracas sépulcral et noir du branle-bas.
Sont-ce des cormorans? sont-ce des citadelles?
Les voiles font un vaste et sourd battement d'ailes;
L'eau gronde, et tout ce groupe énorme vogue, et fuit,
Et s'enfle et roule avec un prodigieux bruit.
Et le lugubre roi sourit de voir groupées
Sur quatre cents vaisseaux quatrevingt mille épées.
O rictus du vampire assouvissant sa faim!
Cette pâle Angleterre, il la tient donc enfin!
Qui pourrait la sauver? Le feu va prendre aux poudres.
Philippe dans sa droite a la gerbe des foudres;
Qui pourrait délier ce faisceau dans son poing?
N'est-il pas le seigneur qu'on ne contredit point?
N'est-il pas l'héritier de César? le Philippe
Dont l'ombre immense va du Gange au Pausilippe?
Tout n'est-il pas fini quand il a dit: Je veux!
N'est-ce pas lui qui tient la victoire aux cheveux?
N'est-ce pas lui qui lance en avant cette flotte,
Ces vaisseaux effrayants dont il est le pilote
Et que la mer charrie ainsi qu'elle le doit?
Ne fait-il pas mouvoir avec son petit doigt
Tous ces dragons ailés et noirs, essaim sans nombre?

N'est-il pas, lui, le roi? n'est-il pas l'homme sombre
A qui ce tourbillon de monstres obéit?

Quand Béit-Cifresil, fils d'Abdallah-Béit,
Eut creusé le grand puits de la mosquée, au Caire,
Il y grava: «Le ciel est à Dieu; j'ai la terre.»
Et, comme tout se tient, se mêle et se confond,
Tous les tyrans n'étant qu'un seul despote au fond,
Ce que dit ce sultan jadis, ce roi le pense.

Cependant, sur le bord du bassin, en silence,
L'infante tient toujours sa rose gravement,
Et, doux ange aux yeux bleus, la baise par moment.
Soudain un souffle d'air, une de ces haleines
Que le soir frémissant jette à travers les plaines,
Tumultueux zéphyr effleurant l'horizon,
Trouble l'eau, fait frémir les joncs, met un frisson
Dans les lointains massifs de myrte et d'asphodèle,
Vient jusqu'au bel enfant tranquille, et, d'un coup d'aile,
Rapide, et secouant même l'arbre voisin,
Effeuille brusquement la fleur dans le bassin.
Et l'infante n'a plus dans la main qu'une épine.
Elle se penche, et voit sur l'eau cette ruine;
Elle ne comprend pas; qu'est-ce donc? Elle a peur;
Et la voilà qui cherche au ciel avec stupeur
Cette brise qui n'a pas craint de lui déplaire.
Que faire? le bassin semble plein de colère;
Lui, si clair tout à l'heure, il est noir maintenant;
Il a des vagues; c'est une mer bouillonnant;
Toute la pauvre rose est éparse sur l'onde;
Ses cent feuilles, que noie et roule l'eau profonde,
Tournoyant, naufrageant, s'en vont de tous côtés
Sur mille petits flots par la brise irrités;
On croit voir dans un gouffre une flotte qui sombre.
«Madame, dit la duègne avec sa face d'ombre
A la petite fille étonnée et rêvant,
Tout sur terre appartient aux princes, hors le vent.»

23 mai 1859

Après la bataille

Mon père, ce héros au sourire si doux,
Suivi d'un seul housard qu'il aimait entre tous
Pour sa grande bravoure et pour sa haute taille,
Parcourait à cheval, le soir d'une bataille,
Le champ couvert de morts sur qui tombait la nuit.
Il lui sembla dans l'ombre entendre un faible bruit.
C'était un Espagnol de l'armée en déroute
Qui se traînait sanglant sur le bord de la route,
Râlant, brisé, livide, et mort plus qu'à moitié,
Et qui disait: «A boire! à boire par pitié!»
Mon père, ému, tendit à son housard fidèle
Une gourde de rhum qui pendait à sa selle,
Et dit: «Tiens, donne à boire à ce pauvre blessé.»
Tout à coup, au moment où le housard baissé
Se penchait vers lui, l'homme, une espèce de Maure,
Saisit un pistolet qu'il étreignait encore,
Et vise au front mon père en criant: Caramba!
Le coup passa si près que le chapeau tomba
Et que le cheval fit un écart en arrière.
«Donne-lui tout de même à boire», dit mon père.

18 juin 1850

Ordre du jour de floréal

Victoire, amis! je dépêche
En hâte et de grand matin
Une strophe toute fraîche
Pour crier le bulletin.

J'embouche sur la montagne
La trompette aux longs éclats;
Sachez que le printemps gagne
La bataille des lilas.

Jeanne met dans sa pantoufle
Son pied qui n'est plus frileux;
Et voici qu'un vaste souffle
Emplit les abîmes bleus.

L'oiseau chante, l'agneau broute;
Mai, poussant des cris railleurs,
Crible l'hiver en déroute
D'une mitraille de fleurs.

Rosa fâchée

Une querelle. Pourquoi?
Mon Dieu! parce qu'on s'adore.
A peine s'est-on dit Toi
Que Vous se hâte d'éclore.

Le cœur tire sur son nœud;
L'azur fuit; l'âme est diverse.
L'amour est un ciel, qui pleut
Sur les amoureux à verse.

De même, quand, sans effroi,
Dans la forêt que juin dore,
On va rôder, sur la foi
Des promesses de l'aurore,

On peut être pris le soir,
Car le beau temps souvent triche,
Par un gros nuage noir
Qui n'était pas sur l'affiche.

Saison des semailles. Le soir

C'est le moment crépusculaire.
J'admire, assis sous un portail,
Ce reste de jour dont s'éclaire
La dernière heure du travail.

Dans les terres, de nuit baignées,
Je contemple, ému, les haillons
D'un vieillard qui jette à poignées
La moisson future aux sillons.

Sa haute silhouette noire
Domine les profonds labours.
On sent à quel point il doit croire
A la fuite utile des jours.

Il marche dans la plaine immense,
Va, vient, lance la graine au loin,
Rouvre sa main, et recommence,
Et je médite, obscur témoin,

Pendant que, déployant ses voiles,
L'ombre, où se mêle une rumeur,
Semble élargir jusqu'aux étoiles
Le geste auguste du semeur.

'Les enfants lisent, troupe blonde...'

Les enfants lisent, troupe blonde;
Ils épellent, je les entends;
Et le maître d'école gronde
Dans la lumière du printemps.

J'aperçois l'école entr'ouverte;
Et je rôde au bord des marais;
Toute la grande saison verte
Frissonne au loin dans les forêts.

Tout rit, tout chante; c'est la fête
De l'infini que nous voyons;
La beauté des fleurs semble faite
Avec la candeur des rayons.

J'épelle aussi moi; je me penche
Sur l'immense livre joyeux;
O champs, quel vers que la pervenche!
Quelle strophe que l'aigle, ô cieux!

Mais, mystère! rien n'est sans tache.
Rien! – Qui peut dire par quels nœuds
La végétation rattache
Le lys chaste au chardon hargneux?

Tandis que là-bas siffle un merle,
La sarcelle, des roseaux plats,
Sort, ayant au bec une perle;
Cette perle agonise, hélas!

C'est le poisson qui, tout à l'heure,
Poursuivait l'aragne, courant
Sur sa bleue et vague demeure,
Sinistre monde transparent.

Un coup de fusil dans la haie,
Abois d'un chien; c'est le chasseur.
Et, pensif, je sens une plaie
Parmi toute cette douceur.

Et, sous l'herbe pressant la fange,
Triste passant de ce beau lieu,
Je songe au mal, énigme étrange,
Faute d'orthographe de Dieu.

23 octobre 1859

'Va-t'en, me dit la bise . . .'

– Va-t'en, me dit la bise,
C'est mon tour de chanter. –
Et, tremblante, surprise,
N'osant pas résister,

Fort décontenancée
Devant un Quos ego,
Ma chanson est chassée
Par cette virago.

Pluie. On me congédie
Partout, sur tous les tons.
Fin de la comédie.
Hirondelles, partons.

Grêle et vent. La ramée
Tord ses bras rabougris;
Là-bas fuit la fumée,
Blanche sur le ciel gris.

Une pâle dorure
Jaunit les coteaux froids.
Le trou de ma serrure
Me souffle sur les doigts.

Pendant une maladie

On dit que je suis fort malade,
Ami; j'ai déjà l'œil terni;
Je sens la sinistre accolade
Du squelette de l'infini.

Sitôt levé, je me recouche;
Et je suis comme si j'avais
De la terre au fond de la bouche;
Je trouve le souffle mauvais.

Comme une voile entrant au havre,
Je frissonne; mes pas sont lents,
J'ai froid; la forme du cadavre,
Morne, apparaît sous mes draps blancs.

Mes mains sont en vain réchauffées;
Ma chair comme la neige fond;
Je sens sur mon front des bouffées
De quelque chose de profond;

Est-ce le vent de l'ombre obscure?
Ce vent qui sur Jésus passa!
Est-ce le grand Rien d'Epicure,
Ou le grand Tout de Spinosa?

Les médecins s'en vont moroses;
On parle bas autour de moi,
Et tout penche, et même les choses
Ont l'attitude de l'effroi.

Perdu! voilà ce qu'on murmure.
Tout mon corps vacille, et je sens
Se déclouer la sombre armure
De ma raison et de mes sens.

Je vois l'immense instant suprême
Dans les ténèbres arriver.
L'astre pâle au fond du ciel blême
Dessine son vague lever.

L'heure réelle, ou décevante,
Dresse son front mystérieux.
Ne crois pas que je m'épouvante;
J'ai toujours été curieux.

Mon âme se change en prunelle;
Ma raison sonde Dieu voilé;
Je tâte la porte éternelle,
Et j'essaie à la nuit ma clé.

C'est Dieu que le fossoyeur creuse;
Mourir, c'est l'heure de savoir;
Je dis à la mort: Vieille ouvreuse,
Je viens voir le spectacle noir.

3 octobre 1859

A l'enfant malade pendant le siège

Si vous continuez d'être ainsi toute pâle
    Dans notre air étouffant,
Si je vous vois entrer dans mon ombre fatale,
    Moi vieillard, vous enfant;

Si je vois de nos jours se confondre la chaîne,
    Moi qui sur mes genoux
Vous contemple, et qui veux la mort pour moi prochaine,
    Et lointaine pour vous;

Si vos mains sont toujours diaphanes et frêles,
    Si, dans votre berceau,
Tremblante, vous avez l'air d'attendre des ailes
    Comme un petit oiseau;

Si vous ne semblez pas prendre sur notre terre
    Racine pour longtemps,
Si vous laissez errer, Jeanne, en notre mystère
    Vos doux yeux mécontents,

Si je ne vous vois pas gaie et rose et très forte,
    Si, triste, vous rêvez,
Si vous ne fermez pas derrière vous la porte
    Par où vous arrivez;

Si je ne vous vois pas comme une belle femme
    Marcher, vous bien porter,
Rire, et si vous semblez être une petite âme
    Qui ne veut pas rester,

Je croirai qu'en ce monde où le suaire au lange
    Parfois peut confiner,
Vous venez pour partir, et que vous êtes l'ange
    Chargé de m'emmener.

A qui la faute?

Tu viens d'incendier la Bibliothèque?
                                        – Oui.
J'ai mis le feu là.
                    – Mais c'est un crime inouï!
Crime commis par toi contre toi-même, infâme!
Mais tu viens de tuer le rayon de ton âme!
C'est ton propre flambeau que tu viens de souffler!
Ce que ta rage impie et folle ose brûler,
C'est ton bien, ton trésor, ta dot, ton héritage!
Le livre, hostile au maître, est à ton avantage.
Le livre a toujours pris fait et cause pour toi.
Une bibliothèque est un acte de foi
Des générations ténébreuses encore
Qui rendent dans la nuit témoignage à l'aurore.
Quoi! dans ce vénérable amas de vérités,
Dans ces chefs-d'œuvre pleins de foudre et de clartés,
Dans ce tombeau des temps devenu répertoire,
Dans les siècles, dans l'homme antique, dans l'histoire,
Dans le passé, leçon qu'épelle l'avenir,
Dans ce qui commença pour ne jamais finir,
Dans les poètes! quoi, dans ce gouffre des bibles,
Dans le divin monceau des Eschyles terribles,
Des Homères, des Jobs, debout sur l'horizon,
Dans Molière, Voltaire et Kant, dans la raison,
Tu jettes, misérable, une torche enflammée!
De tout l'esprit humain tu fais de la fumée!
As-tu donc oublié que ton libérateur,
C'est le livre? Le livre est là sur la hauteur;
Il luit; parce qu'il brille et qu'il les illumine,
Il détruit l'échafaud, la guerre, la famine;
Il parle, plus d'esclave et plus de paria.
Ouvre un livre, Platon, Milton, Beccaria;
Lis ces prophètes, Dante, ou Shakspeare, ou Corneille;
L'âme immense qu'ils ont en eux, en toi s'éveille;
Ébloui, tu te sens le même homme qu'eux tous;
Tu deviens en lisant grave, pensif et doux;
Tu sens dans ton esprit tous ces grands hommes croître,
Ils t'enseignent ainsi que l'aube éclaire un cloître;
A mesure qu'il plonge en ton cœur plus avant,
Leur chaud rayon t'apaise et te fait plus vivant;
Ton âme interrogée est prête à leur répondre;
Tu te reconnais bon, puis meilleur; tu sens fondre
Comme la neige au feu, ton orgueil, tes fureurs,
Le mal, les préjugés, les rois, les empereurs!
Car la science en l'homme arrive la première.

Puis vient la liberté. Toute cette lumière,
C'est à toi, comprends donc, et c'est toi qui l'éteins!
Les buts rêvés par toi sont par le livre atteints!
Le livre en ta pensée entre, il défait en elle
Les liens que l'erreur à la vérité mêle,
Car toute conscience est un nœud gordien.
Il est ton médecin, ton guide, ton gardien.
Ta haine, il la guérit; ta démence, il te l'ôte.
Voilà ce que tu perds, hélas, et par ta faute!
Le livre est ta richesse à toi! c'est le savoir,
Le droit, la vérité, la vertu, le devoir,
Le progrès, la raison dissipant tout délire.
Et tu détruis cela, toi!
                – Je ne sais pas lire.

Juin 1871

A Théophile Gautier

Ami, poète, esprit, tu fuis notre nuit noire.
Tu sors de nos rumeurs pour entrer dans la gloire;
Et désormais ton nom rayonne aux purs sommets.
Moi qui t'ai connu jeune et beau, moi qui t'aimais,
Moi qui, plus d'une fois, dans nos altiers coups d'aile,
Éperdu, m'appuyais sur ton âme fidèle,
Moi, blanchi par les jours sur ma tête neigeant,
Je me souviens des temps écoulés, et songeant
A ce jeune passé qui vit nos deux aurores,
A la lutte, à l'orage, aux arènes sonores,
A l'art nouveau qui s'offre, au peuple criant: oui,
J'écoute ce grand vent sublime évanoui.

         *

Fils de la Grèce antique et de la jeune France,
Ton fier respect des morts fut rempli d'espérance;
Jamais tu ne fermas les yeux à l'avenir.
Mage à Thèbes, druide au pied du noir menhir,
Flamine aux bords du Tibre et brahme aux bords du Gange,
Mettant sur l'arc du dieu la flèche de l'archange,
D'Achille et de Roland hantant les deux chevets,
Forgeur mystérieux et puissant, tu savais
Tordre tous les rayons dans une seule flamme;
Le couchant rencontrait l'aurore dans ton âme;
Hier croisait demain dans ton fécond cerveau;
Tu sacrais le vieil art aïeul de l'art nouveau;
Tu comprenais qu'il faut, lorsqu'une âme inconnue
Parle au peuple, envolée en éclairs dans la nue,
L'écouter, l'accepter, l'aimer, ouvrir les cœurs;
Calme, tu dédaignais l'effort vil des moqueurs
Écumant sur Eschyle et bavant sur Shakspeare;
Tu savais que ce siècle a son air qu'il respire,
Et que, l'art ne marchant qu'en se transfigurant,
C'est embellir le beau que d'y joindre le grand.
Et l'on t'a vu pousser d'illustres cris de joie
Quand le Drame a saisi Paris comme une proie,
Quand l'antique hiver fut chassé par Floréal,
Quand l'astre inattendu du moderne idéal
Est venu tout à coup, dans le ciel qui s'embrase
Luire, et quand l'Hippogriffe a relayé Pégase!

　　　　*

Je te salue au seuil sévère du tombeau.
Va chercher le vrai, toi qui sus trouver le beau.
Monte l'âpre escalier. Du haut des sombres marches,
Du noir pont de l'abîme on entrevoit les arches;
Va! meurs! la dernière heure est le dernier degré.
Pars, aigle, tu vas voir des gouffres à ton gré;
Tu vas voir l'absolu, le réel, le sublime.
Tu vas sentir le vent sinistre de la cime
Et l'éblouissement du prodige éternel.
Ton olympe, tu vas le voir du haut du ciel,
Tu vas du haut du vrai voir l'humaine chimère,
Même celle de Job, même celle d'Homère,
Âme, et du haut de Dieu tu vas voir Jéhovah.
Monte, esprit! Grandis, plane, ouvre tes ailes, va!

Lorsqu'un vivant nous quitte, ému, je le contemple;
Car entrer dans la mort, c'est entrer dans le temple
Et quand un homme meurt, je vois distinctement
Dans son ascension mon propre avènement.
Ami, je sens du sort la sombre plénitude;
J'ai commencé la mort par de la solitude,
Je vois mon profond soir vaguement s'étoiler.
Voici l'heure où je vais, aussi moi, m'en aller.
Mon fil trop long frissonne et touche presque au glaive;
Le vent qui t'emporta doucement me soulève,
Et je vais suivre ceux qui m'aimaient, moi banni.
Leur œil fixe m'attire au fond de l'infini.
J'y cours. Ne fermez pas la porte funéraire.

Passons; car c'est la loi; nul ne peut s'y soustraire;
Tout penche; et ce grand siècle avec tous ses rayons
Entre en cette ombre immense où pâles nous fuyons.
Oh! quel farouche bruit font dans le crépuscule
Les chênes qu'on abat pour le bûcher d'Hercule!
Les chevaux de la mort se mettent à hennir,
Et sont joyeux, car l'âge éclatant va finir;
Ce siècle altier qui sut dompter le vent contraire,
Expire . . . – Ô Gautier! toi, leur égal et leur frère,
Tu pars après Dumas, Lamartine et Musset.
L'onde antique est tarie où l'on rajeunissait;
Comme il n'est plus de Styx il n'est plus de Jouvence.
Le dur faucheur avec sa large lame avance
Pensif et pas à pas vers le reste du blé;
C'est mon tour; et la nuit emplit mon œil troublé
Qui, devinant, hélas, l'avenir des colombes,
Pleure sur des berceaux et sourit à des tombes.

2 novembre 1872. Jour des Morts

[*pp.* 144–145]

Orphée

J'atteste Tanaïs, le noir fleuve aux six urnes,
Et Zeus qui fait traîner sur les grands chars nocturnes
Rhéa par des taureaux et Nyx par des chevaux,
Et les anciens géants et les hommes nouveaux,
Pluton qui nous dévore, Uranus qui nous crée,
Que j'adore une femme et qu'elle m'est sacrée.
Le monstre aux cheveux bleus, Poséidon, m'entend;
Qu'il m'exauce. Je suis l'âme humaine chantant,
Et j'aime. L'ombre immense est pleine de nuées,
La large pluie abonde aux feuilles remuées,
Borée émeut les bois, Zéphyre émeut les blés,
Ainsi nos cœurs profonds sont par l'amour troublés.
J'aimerai cette femme appelée Eurydice
Toujours, partout! Sinon que le ciel me maudisse,
Et maudisse la fleur naissante et l'épi mûr!
Ne tracez pas de mots magiques sur le mur.

3 février 1877

Après les fourches caudines

Rome avait trop de gloire, ô dieux, vous la punîtes
Par le triomphe énorme et lâche des samnites;
Et nous vîmes ce deuil, nous qui vivons encor.
Cela n'empêche pas l'aurore aux rayons d'or
D'éclore et d'apparaître au-dessus des collines.
Un champ de course est près des tombes Esquilines,
Et parfois, quand la foule y fourmille en tous sens,
J'y vais, l'œil vaguement fixé sur les passants.
Ce champ mène aux logis de guerre, où les cohortes
Vont et viennent ainsi que dans les villes fortes;
Avril sourit, l'oiseau chante, et, dans le lointain,
Derrière les coteaux où reluit le matin,
Où les roses des bois entr'ouvrent leurs pétales,
On entend murmurer les trompettes fatales;
Et je médite, ému. J'étais aujourd'hui là.
Je ne sais pas pourquoi le soleil se voila;
Les nuages parfois dans le ciel se resserrent.
Tout à coup, à cheval et lance au poing, passèrent
Des vétérans aux fronts hâlés, aux larges mains;
Ils avaient l'ancien air des grands soldats romains;
Et les petits enfants accouraient pour les suivre;
Trois cavaliers, soufflant dans des buccins de cuivre,
Marchaient en tête, et comme, au front de l'escadron,
Chacun d'eux embouchait à son tour le clairon,
Sans couper la fanfare, ils reprenaient haleine.
Ces gens de guerre étaient superbes dans la plaine;
Ils marchaient de leur pas antique et souverain.
Leurs boucliers portaient des méduses d'airain,
Et l'on voyait sur eux Gorgone et tous ses masques;
Ils défilaient, dressant les cimiers de leurs casques,
Dignes d'être éclairés par des soleils levants,
Sous des crins de lion qui se tordaient aux vents.
Que ces hommes sont beaux! disaient les jeunes filles.
Tout souriait, les fleurs embaumaient les charmilles,
Le peuple était joyeux, le ciel était doré,
Et, songeant que c'étaient des vaincus, j'ai pleuré.

Fenêtres ouvertes

J'entends des voix. Lueurs à travers ma paupière.
Une cloche est en branle à l'église Saint-Pierre.
Cris des baigneurs: «Plus près! Plus loin! Non, par ici!
Non, par là!» Les oiseaux gazouillent, Jeanne aussi.
Georges l'appelle. Chant des coqs. Une truelle
Racle un toit. Des chevaux passent dans la ruelle.
Grincement d'une faux qui coupe le gazon.
Chocs. Rumeurs. Des couvreurs marchent sur la maison.
Bruits du port. Sifflement des machines chauffées.
Musique militaire arrivant par bouffées.
Brouhaha sur le quai. Voix françaises. «Merci.
Bonjour. Adieu.» Sans doute, il est tard, car voici
Que vient tout près de moi chanter mon rouge-gorge.
Vacarme de marteaux lointains dans une forge.
L'eau clapote. On entend haleter un steamer.
Une mouche entre. Souffle immense de la mer.

'Jeanne songeait...'

Jeanne songeait, sur l'herbe assise, grave et rose;
Je m'approchai: – Dis-moi si tu veux quelque chose,
Jeanne. – Car j'obéis à ces charmants amours,
Je les guette, et je cherche à comprendre toujours
Tout ce qui peut passer par ces divines têtes.
Jeanne m'a répondu: – Je voudrais voir des bêtes.
Alors je lui montrai dans l'herbe une fourmi.
Vois! – Mais Jeanne ne fut contente qu'à demi.
– Non, les bêtes, c'est gros, me dit-elle.
                                Leur rêve,
C'est le grand. L'océan les attire à sa grève,
Les berçant de son chant rauque, et les captivant
Par l'ombre, et par la fuite effrayante du vent;
Ils aiment l'épouvante, il leur faut le prodige.
– Je n'ai pas d'éléphant sous la main, répondis-je.
Veux-tu quelque autre chose? ô Jeanne, on te le doit,
Parle. – Alors Jeanne au ciel leva son petit doigt.
– Ça, dit-elle. – C'était l'heure où le soir commence.
Je vis à l'horizon surgir la lune immense.

A ma fille Adèle

Tout enfant, tu dormais près de moi, rose et fraîche,
Comme un petit Jésus accroupi dans la crèche;
Ton pur sommeil était si calme et si charmant
Que tu n'entendais pas l'oiseau chanter dans l'ombre;
Moi, pensif, j'aspirais toute la douceur sombre
    Du mystérieux firmament.

Et j'écoutais voler sur ta tête les anges;
Et je te regardais dormir; et sur tes langes
J'effeuillais des jasmins et des œillets sans bruit;
Et je priais, veillant sur tes paupières closes;
Et mes yeux se mouillaient de pleurs, songeant aux choses
    Qui nous attendent dans la nuit.

Un jour mon tour viendra de dormir, et ma couche,
Faite d'ombre, sera si morne et si farouche
Que je n'entendrai pas non plus chanter l'oiseau;
Et la nuit sera noire; alors, ô ma colombe,
Larmes, prière et fleurs, tu rendras à ma tombe
    Ce que j'ai fait pour ton berceau.

4 octobre 1857

Notes

The poems are printed in chronological order of publication.

IN THE VALLEY OF CHERIZY (p. 27)
  The death of V.H.'s mother in June 1821 probably explains the 'shadow in the past' and the use of 'orphaned'. M. Foucher had forbidden his daughter to see V.H. and so the poet travelled on foot to their house at Dreux, some fifty miles west of Paris, passing through the valley of Cherizy where this poem is set.

MORNING (p. 30)
  In March 1822 M. Foucher consented to the marriage.
  The French text is that of the 1829 edition. Later editions carry variant readings of two lines in verse two:
  line 3   Un soleil aussi beau luire à ton désespoir,
  line 5   Sur mon tombeau muet et noir!

THE BOY (p. 31)
  This is, perhaps via Delacroix's painting, a reference to the Turkish massacre of 25,000 Chiotes in 1822.

OLYMPIO: HIS SADNESS (p. 56)
  'Olympio' was V.H.'s name for himself as poet.

THE SONG OF THOSE WHO GO TO SEA (p. 63)
  V.H. wrote this poem crossing the Channel when the Belgian authorities had expelled him following the publication of *Napoléon-le-petit*.

THE HUNTSMAN OF THE NIGHT (p. 64)
  The idea of the wild huntsman is common in German literature and V.H. is drawing on recollections of poems by Bürger and others while using the 'huntsman' as a symbol of Republican France.

THE RETREAT FROM MOSCOW (p. 67)

This is the first section of a long poem entitled *L'expiation*. Napoleon I is atoning for the crime he committed when he took the title of First Consul. This V.H. regarded as the first step on the road to becoming emperor, hence betraying the republic. The final grotesque punishment will be a vision of his nephew establishing the Second Empire.

A RECOLLECTION OF THE NIGHT OF 4 DECEMBER 1851 (p. 70)

On 2 December 1851 Louis-Napoléon proclaimed himself Emperor of the French. Two days later he sent troops to fire on a crowd of demonstrators, killing hundreds of onlookers including women and children. V.H.'s poem commemorates a boy of seven killed that day in the Rue Tiquetonne.

CHILDHOOD (p. 77)

Mme Ginestat, a neighbour of V.H.'s on Jersey, died of tuberculosis in January 1855, leaving a small son. With only three exceptions, the poems in Books I and III of *Les Contemplations* written after 4 September 1843 are given a fictive date well prior to the death of Léopoldine, reactions to which will dominate Book IV. Here, a poem juxtaposing death and a young child (mortality, as it were, foreshadowing the death of Léopoldine) is included unusually among the poems in Book I and given a date 20 years before the event which inspired it.

UNITY (p. 78)

V.H. is recalling Correggio's remark before a painting of Raphael's – 'Anch'io son' pittore', 'I am a painter too.'

THE FIRST OF MAY (p. 79)

This is the first poem in Book II of *Les Contemplations*, which consists entirely of love poems mostly addressed to Juliette. For perhaps tactful reasons these poems, unlike those in the other five books, are given no specific dates.

It is interesting to compare the part played by memory at the conclusion of 'Olympio: His Sadness' with that in 'One Evening When I Was Looking at the Sky.' Also to realize in the latter poem as well as in 'Words Spoken in the Shadows' that V.H. – occasionally – was capable of a compassionate view of Juliette's often thankless rôle.

QUEEN OMPHALÉ'S SPINNING-WHEEL (p. 80)
Hercules/Hugo is perhaps explaining his enslavement to Omphalé/Juliette and they are probably 'off-stage' making love. The depiction of Europa however would seem to convey a different emphasis on their relationship; cf. 'Words Spoken in the Shadows' and 'One Evening When I Was Looking at the Sky'.

ON THE PLINTH OF AN ANCIENT BAS-RELIEF (p. 89)
The dedication is to Mlle Louise Bertin, composer of the opera *Esmeralda* based on Hugo's *Notre-Dame de Paris.*

'AT DAWN, TOMORROW . . .' (p. 100)
V.H. is planning a pilgrimage to his daughter's grave at Villequier on the fourth anniversary of her death.

SHEPHERDS AND THEIR FLOCKS (p. 103)
The dedication is to Mme Louise Colet, a poet, who living in France dealt with correspondence for V.H. in exile.

CHRIST'S FIRST ENCOUNTER WITH THE TOMB (p. 120)
Technically neither Elijah nor Job spoke in parables: a curious mistake of V.H.'s, for he read the Bible constantly. Also, more excusably, he misunderstood the length of a 'stade', thus making Bethany, one mile out of Jerusalem, a three-day journey!

THE ROSE IN THE INFANTA'S HAND (p. 123)
V.H. is in an interesting dilemma here for the Infanta is a child, therefore pure, but also a future ruler, therefore evil. The interplay of images and attitudes between his depiction of the little girl and of Philip II make the poem a masterly construction of parallels.

Successive reprints of this poem have perpetrated a curious error – 'navires' for 'vaisseaux' in line 198: the former word, having three syllables in verse, would not scan.

Béit-Cifresil seems to have been an invention of V.H.'s.

TO THÉOPHILE GAUTIER (p. 143)

This was published in 1873 at the head of a collection of poems in memory of Gautier. In 1888 it was included in the posthumous volume *Toute la lyre*.

AFTER THE CAUDINE FORKS (p. 147)

In 321 B.C. the Samnite army defeated the Romans at the Caudine Forks. V.H. is writing a historical piece but Rome is easily seen as Paris after France's defeat in the Franco-Prussian War.

Bibliography

The definitive text for all Hugo's work is still the *Œuvres complètes* in 45 volumes brought out between 1904 and 1952 by the Imprimerie Nationale.

There is another edition of the complete works in 18 volumes published in 1967 by Le Club français du livre. Two further publications have produced the poetry alone: *Œuvres poétiques complètes*, (Pauvert, Paris, 1961: one volume) and *Poésie* (Editions du Seuil, Paris, 1972: three volumes). The Pléïade edition (1950–1974) is the full critical edition of the poems published in Hugo's lifetime although some of the work collected posthumously has not yet appeared in this series. There are adequate cheap editions of most of Hugo's work in verse published by Garnier-Flammarion, Livre de poche and Classiques Larousse – these last are heavily, often usefully, annotated but the longer poems tend to be severely truncated with whole sections summarized in prose. More scholarly editions appear from Classiques Garnier.

Biographies in English include:

Mathew Josephson, *Victor Hugo*. Doubleday, 1942
André Maurois (tr. Gerard Hopkins), *Victor Hugo*. Jonathan Cape, 1956
Joanna Richardson, *Victor Hugo*. Weidenfeld & Nicolson, 1976

Other works in English include:

G. Barnett Smith, *Victor Hugo, His Life and Work*. Ward & Downey, 1885
A.C. Swinburne, *A Study of Victor Hugo*. Chatto & Windus, 1886
Memoirs of Victor Hugo translated by John W. Harding. Heinemann, 1899
A.F. Davidson, *Victor Hugo, His Life and Works*. Eveleigh Nash, 1912
Elliott M. Grant, *The Career of Victor Hugo*. Harvard, 1946
André Maurois (tr. Oliver Bernard), *Victor Hugo and His World*. Thames & Hudson, 1966

Richard B. Grant, *The Perilous Quest*. Duke University Press, 1968

C.W. Thompson, *Victor Hugo and the Graphic Arts*. Droz, Geneva, 1970

John Porter Houston, *Victor Hugo*. Twayne, 1974

There are three good editions of Hugo's graphic works:

Dessins de Victor Hugo présentés par J. Sergent. La Palatine, Paris, 1955

Victor Hugo dessinateur, notes et légendes de Roger Cornaille et Georges Herscher. Editions du Minotaure, Paris, 1963

Shadows of a Hand, The Drawings of Victor Hugo, The Drawing Center, New York in association with Merrell Holberton Publishers, London, 1998

Chronological Table

1802   February 26th, birth of V. H. at Besançon

1803   Birth of Adèle Foucher (Mme Victor Hugo) at Paris

1806   Birth of Julienne Gauvain (Juliette Drouet) at Fougères

1808   Separation of V.H.'s parents

1821   Death of V.H.'s mother

1822   After two years of opposition M. Foucher consents to the marriage of V.H. to his daughter
      Odes et Poésies diverses

1823   Eugène, born 1800, V.H.'s brother, certified insane
      Death of Léopold, V.H.'s son, aged 3 months

1824   Birth of Léopoldine

1825   Invitation to the coronation of Charles X
      Légion d'honneur

1826   Birth of Charles
      Odes et Ballades

1827   Meeting with Sainte-Beuve
      Cromwell with the preface that is to become a manifesto of the romantic school

1828   Death of General Hugo
      Birth of François-Victor

1829   *Les Orientales*
      Marion de Lorme banned by Charles X

1830   *Hernani* performed amid riots at the Théâtre-Français
      Birth of Adèle
      Sainte-Beuve's confession of love for Mme V.H.

1831   *Notre-Dame de Paris*
      Les Feuilles d'automne

1832   *Le Roi s'amuse* banned

1833   Meeting with Juliette Drouet

1835   *Les Chants du crépuscule*

1837   Death of Eugène in the insane asylum at Charenton
      Les Voix intérieures

1838   *Ruy Blas*

1840   *Les Rayons et les Ombres*

1841   V.H. elected to the Académie Française having been rejected three times

1843	Marriage of Léopoldine with Charles Vacquerie in February
	Failure of *Les Burgraves* at the Théâtre-Français in March
	Léopoldine and Charles drowned at Villequier in September
1848	V.H. elected deputy; founds the newspaper *L'Événement*
1851	*Rigoletto* based on *Le Roi s'amuse* performed
	L'Événement banned and V.H.'s two sons arrested
	After Louis-Napoléon's coup d'état V.H. tries to organize resistance and is forced to flee in disguise to Brussels: his passport, procured by Juliette, claimed he was a typographer called Jacques-Firmin Lanvin
1852	Formal exile declared
	Napoléon-le-petit
	V.H. installed on Jersey
1853	*Les Châtiments*
1855	Death of V.H.'s brother Abel, born 1798
	V.H. expelled from Jersey for having sided with other exiles attacking the Franco-British alliance: moves to Guernsey
1856	*Les Contemplations*
1858	V.H. gravely ill
1859	Napoleon III pronounces amnesty – refused by V.H.
	La Légende des siècles (1st series)
1862	*Les Misérables*
	V.H.'s drawings published in one volume
1863	Adèle falls in love with an officer named Pinson and goes insane on learning he is married
1865	Marriage of Charles
	Les Chansons des rues et des bois
1866	*Les Travailleurs de la mer*
1867	Birth of Georges, V.H.'s first grandchild
1868	Death of Georges in April
	Birth in August of Charles Hugo's second son, also christened Georges
	Death of Mme V.H.
1869	Birth of Jeanne, V.H.'s grand-daughter
1870	V.H. returns to Paris on proclamation of Third Republic
	First French edition of *Les Châtiments*

1871	V.H. elected deputy
	Death of Charles
	V.H. leaves for Belgium, offers asylum to Communards, is expelled from Belgium, moves to Luxembourg, returns to Paris in September
1872	*L'Année terrible*
1873	Death of François-Victor
1876	V.H. elected senator
1877	*La Légende des siècles* (2nd series)
	L'Art d'être grand-père
1878	*Le Pape*
1879	*La Pitié suprême*
1880	*Religions et Religion*
	L'Âne
1881	*Les Quatre vents de l'esprit*
1882	*Le Roi s'amuse* performed after 50 years
1883	Death of Juliette Drouet
	La Légende des siècles (3rd series)
1885	May 22nd, death of V.H.

Index of French Titles

A Albert Dürer, 170
A l'enfant malade pendant le siège, 228
A ma fille Adèle, 236
A qui la faute?, 229
'A quoi je songe . . . ?', 171
A Théophile Gautier, 231
A un voyageur, 160
Après la bataille, 222
Après les fourches caudines, 234
Attente, 158

Booz endormi, 211

Ce que c'est que la mort, 204

'Demain, dès l'aube . . .', 200

Écrit au bas d'un crucifix, 194
Écrit sur la plinthe d'un bas-relief antique, 194
'Elle avait pris ce pli . . .', 197

Fenêtres ouvertes, 235

'J'aime l'araignée . . .', 196
'Jeanne songeait . . .', 235

'La clarté du dehors . . .', 195
'L'aurore s'allume . . .', 168
L'enfance, 187
L'enfant, 157
'L'enfant, voyant l'aïeule . . .', 196
L'expiation, 1, 182
La conscience, 210
La rose de l'infante, 216
Le chant de ceux qui s'en vont sur mer, 179
Le chasseur noir, 180
Le matin, 157
Le rouet d'Omphale, 189
Le sacre de la femme, 205
'Les enfants lisent, troupe blonde. . .', 224
Lettre, 190

'Lorsque l'enfant paraît . . .', 163

Mes deux filles, 185

Napoléon II (*extrait*), 166
Nomen, numen, lumen, 204
Nuits de juin, 173

Oceano nox, 172
'Oh! qui que vous soyez . . .', 164
Ordre du jour de floréal, 222
Orphée, 233

Paroles dans l'ombre, 191
Paroles sur la dune, 201
Pasteurs et troupeaux, 202
Pendant une maladie, 226
Premier mai, 188
Première rencontre du Christ avec le tombeau, 214
'Puisque j'ai mis ma lèvre . . .', 169

'Quand nous habitions tous ensemble . . .', 198

Rêverie, 159
Rosa fâchée, 223

Saison des semailles. Le soir, 224
Soleils couchants, vi, 160
'Sonnez, sonnez toujours . . .', 185
Souvenir de la nuit du 4, 183
Sur le bal de l'Hôtel de Ville, 166

Tristesse d'Olympio, 174

Un soir que je regardais le ciel, 192
Unité, 188

'Va-t'en, me dit la bise . . .', 226
Veni, vidi, vixi, 199
Vieille chanson du jeune temps, 186
'Viens! – une flûte invisible . . .', 191

Index of English Titles

'A little girl . . .', 92
After the Battle, 131
After the Caudine Forks, 147
'At dawn, tomorrow . . .', 100

Boaz Asleep, 117
The Boy, 31

'Come – an unseen flute . . .', 84
The Child Appears, 39
Childhood, 77
Christ's First Encounter with the Tomb, 120
Concerning the Ball at the Hôtel de Ville, 45
Conscience, 115
The Consecration of Woman, 107

'Dawn is igniting . . .', 47
During an Illness, 138

The First of May, 79

The Huntsman of the Night, 64

For Jeanne, Ill During the Siege of Paris, 140

Grand-daughter, 150

June Nights, 55

'Let all the bugles . . .', 73
Letter, 82

Morning, 30
My Thoughts, 51
My Two Daughters, 74

Night on the Ocean, 53
Nomen, Numen, Lumen, 106

Old Song of my Young Days, 75
Olympio: His Sadness, 56
On the Plinth of an Ancient Bas-Relief, 89
'On our hills of the past . . .', 96

One Evening When I Was Looking at the Sky, 86
Onset of Winter, 134
Open Windows: Early Morning, 149
Orders for the Day: Late Spring, 132
Orpheus, 146

Queen Omphalé's Spinning-Wheel, 80

A Recollection of the Night of 4 December 1851, 70
The Retreat from Moscow, 67
Reverie, 34
Rosa's Angry, 133
The Rose in the Infanta's Hand, 123

'She formed the habit . . .', 95
Shepherds and Their Flocks, 103
'Since I have placed my lip . . .', 48
The Song of Those Who Go to Sea, 63
The Sower, 134
'Spider, nettle, loathed . . .', 93
Sunset, 35

'The bright air outside . . .', 90
'The children read . . .', 135
To a Traveller, 36
To Albrecht Dürer, 49
To My Daughter Adèle, 151
To Théophile Gautier, 143
Tomorrow, 44

Unity, 78

Veni, Vidi, Vixi, 98

Waiting, 33
What Death Is, 105
'Whoever you may be . . .', 42
Whose Fault Is It?, 141
Words Spoken in the Shadows, 85
Words Spoken on the Dunes, 101
Written Beneath a Crucifix, 88

French Poetry in Bilingual Editions from Anvil

Guillaume Apollinaire: Selected Poems
Translated and introduced by Oliver Bernard

A cross-section of the most dynamic modernist French poet's work. 'Oliver Bernard's translations . . . are immediately engaging in their vividness and humour.'
Christopher Ricks, *New Statesman*

Charles Baudelaire
Translated and introduced by Francis Scarfe
Volume I: The Complete Verse
Volume II: The Poems in Prose *with 'La Fanfarlo'*

Francis Scarfe's prose versions of the complete poetry of France's greatest nineteenth-century poet are both scrupulous and inventive. 'No one must underestimate the value of the present enterprise to even the most advanced student of French literature.'
Michael Glover, *British Book News*

Poems of Jules Laforgue
Translated and introduced by Peter Dale

Peter Dale captures Laforgue's wit and panache in this substantial selection from one of the quirkiest and most entertaining of French poets. 'Generally, when Dale adapts, he still manages to reproduce, conveying much of the letter of the original as well as the spirit. . . . The collection is hard to over-praise' – D.J. Enright, *The Observer*

Gérard de Nerval: The Chimeras
Translated by Peter Jay
with an essay by Richard Holmes

'The rendering of Gérard de Nerval's justly celebrated and mysteriously allusive sonnet sequence in English is a formidably difficult enterprise, and translator and publisher are to be congratulated.'

Michael Glover, *Books and Bookmen*

Arthur Rimbaud: A Season in Hell
and Other Poems
Translated by Norman Cameron
with an introduction by Michael Hamburger

In the opinion of Robert Graves, Norman Cameron was unsurpassed as a translator of Rimbaud. This volume contains thirty-three of the verse poems and the whole of *Une Saison en enfer*, the extraordinary work that was Rimbaud's literary testament, his apology, and a contribution to the mythology of his time.

Paul Verlaine: Women/Men
Translated by Alistair Elliot

'. . . in Verlaine's clandestine collections of erotic verse, Mr Elliot succeeds marvellously . . . astonishing, beautiful poems, astonishingly and beautifully rendered.' — D. M. Thomas

Poems of François Villon
Translated and introduced by Peter Dale

Peter Dale's remarkable translation is now reissued in this much revised bilingual edition. Holding close to Villon's rhyme-schemes and metres, he gives us the vigour, wit and charm of this fascinating medieval poet.

Poetica

Some other titles in this series of texts, translations
and other works relating to poetry

2   The Noise Made by Poems   *Peter Levi*

3   The Satires of Persius   *W. S. Merwin*

4   Flower and Song: Aztec Poems   *Edward Kissam*
    & Michael Schmidt

5   Palladas: Poems   *Tony Harrison*

6   The Song of Songs   *Peter Jay*

11   Old English Riddles   *Michael Alexander*

12   Rilke: Turning-Point (Poems 1912–1926)
     Michael Hamburger

14   Martial: Letter to Juvenal   *Peter Whigham*

15   Li He: Goddesses, Ghosts, and Demons   *J. D. Frodsham*

16   Nietzsche: Dithyrambs of Dionysus   *R. J. Hollingdale*

19   The Lamentation of the Dead   *Peter Levi*

21   Slow Chrysanthemums: Classical Korean Poetry in Chinese
     Kim Jong-gil

23   The Selected Poems of Tu Fu   *David Hinton*

24   Hölderlin Poems and Fragments   *Michael Hamburger*

25   Luis de Góngora: Selected Shorter Poems   *Michael Smith*

26   Borrowed Ware: Medieval Persian Epigrams   *Dick Davis*

27   Sappho Through English Poetry   *Peter Jay*
     and Caroline Lewis (eds.)

28   The Truth of Poetry   *Michael Hamburger*

29   Goethe: Roman Elegies and other poems
     Michael Hamburger

30   Dante: The Divine Comedy   *Peter Dale*

31   The Selected Poems of Li Po   *David Hinton*

33   Yehuda Halevi: Poems from the Diwan   *Gabriel Levin*

34   The Selected Poems of Po Chü-i   *David Hinton*

35   From Russian with Love: Joseph Brodsky in English
     Daniel Weissbort